Praise for *Simplicity Driven Leadership*

"David Liddell has climbed the mountain with many CEOs and senior executives through complex transformations. His book cuts through the noise and identifies common (but not always obvious) leadership and culture problems that hold countless businesses back. David keeps it real with messy stories and gives simple nuggets of advice that, when practically applied, will deliver remarkable results!"

— Renee Zaugg
Former SVP IT CVSH and Global CIO Otis Elevator

"Keeping things simple isn't always so easy. This book, however, strips away the excess to uncover leadership challenges that are common yet not always immediately apparent. Leaders will more fully understand how to focus on the strategic issues that truly matter and will make a timely difference. In addition, each organization, larger or smaller, will better grasp the need for an emotional maturity that filters through the layers of management. Finally, this book highlights the need for team activation and communication techniques and provokes the further topic of the need to renew and refresh your teams.

By the end of this book, you will be able to laser in on the issues affecting your operation, take informed action and realize the company's full potential."

— Andy Griffiths
Former President Samsung UK and Ireland.

"Without a doubt, I would not be where I am today without David Liddell. His philosophies, honesty and unwavering support were instrumental in my path to a career that I frankly never thought was possible for a girl from Muncie, Indiana. I'm so thrilled he has put this incredible approach to leadership and growing business into a book, so everyone has access."

— Melissa Hobley
Global CMO at Tinder (Match Group, Inc.)

"Over the past decade, I've had the privilege of knowing David Liddell, and his support has played a pivotal role in fostering the growth of both our team and business. David's exceptional leadership style sets him apart. He doesn't passively observe but actively engages with the challenges at hand. His coaching expertise and profound business acumen resonate across all organizational levels, perfectly aligning with our mission of fostering leadership scalability and creating sustainable local jobs. David's contributions have not only developed our leaders but also driven our business to become high-performing with a world-class culture. His ability to act as a versatile generalist in both cultural and business leadership has been immensely valuable, especially in our dynamic business environment, where cross-functional collaboration is vital.

I wholeheartedly recommend David's book and strongly urge anyone seeking to enhance talent and consistency within their organization to reach out to David for his invaluable assistance. His wealth of experience and insights is a priceless asset that can undoubtedly propel your organization toward greater success. David's immeasurable contributions to our business gives me confidence that he can do the same for yours."

— Russ Nadeau
COO EPTAM Precision Solutions

Simplicity Driven
Leadership

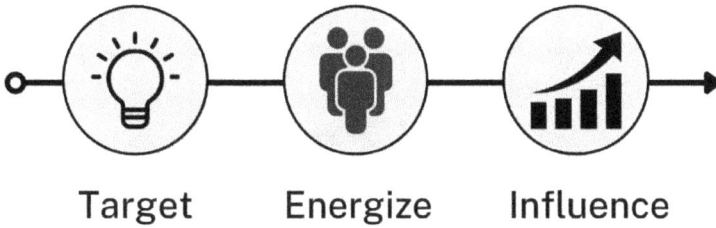

Target   Energize   Influence

To request permissions, contact the author at **David@LiddellConsulting.com**

Cover art and book layout by David Liddell with
Cindy Murphy, Bluemoon Graphics.

Published by ClearPath Press

ISBN: 979-8-9901763-0-0

Simplicity Driven
Leadership

3 Key Principles to Help a Business Thrive

DAVID LIDDELL

For my wife, Cindy

I dedicate this book, with sincerity, to my wife Cindy
who has been an avid supporter of my work and who had the willingness
to tolerate the ups and downs of getting my business started
many years ago. It would not have been possible without her.

And, for my clients

Thank you for believing in me and all the relationships
we have developed together.

TABLE OF CONTENTS

"Simplicity is the ultimate sophistication."
— Leonardo da Vinci

"Any intelligent fool can make things bigger and more complex.
It takes a touch of genius—and a lot of courage—
to move in the opposite direction."
— E.F. Schumacher

Preface

Throughout my life, I've always been able to spot the simplicity in things, even when they appeared complicated. After graduating from university and entering the business world, I found that the same principle applied to organizations. What may seem like a chaotic web of moving parts—multiple functions, processes, and personalities—can often be understood as one interconnected system. Much like the synchronized movement of a school of fish or the mesmerizing patterns of starlings in flight, the key lies in recognizing the simplicity beneath the surface.

The challenge for many of us is perspective. When you're too close, you can get lost in the chaos, overwhelmed by the noise of immediate problems and daily challenges. You see the mess but miss the underlying flow. On the other hand, when you're too far removed, you risk losing touch with the factors that shape the system, the subtle forces influencing behavior and outcomes.

The art of leadership—and, indeed, the art of business—lies in finding the right vantage point. It requires deep thinking, continual learning, and a sharp understanding of what truly drives behavior and results.

All leaders face complications, whether in strategy, people, or process. Yet I believe that while business challenges may seem complicated, they don't have to be. Often, the confusion stems from a lack of clarity in how we approach those challenges. Many leaders, though well-intentioned, end up complicating matters further, not out of negligence, but because they lack a clear framework that offers perspective and direction.

This book presents that framework, built on three foundational principles that can bring order to chaos and help you lead with greater confidence and clarity. In the pages ahead, we'll explore how these principles can transform your leadership.

You will learn how to:

1. Establish clear expectations and build a platform for success
2. Activate and motivate people, master consensus building, and drive team performance
3. Deliver consistent results by fostering a culture of accountability, action, and execution

Through real-world stories and practical applications, you'll see how these principles interlock to form a comprehensive approach to leadership. My goal is for you to walk away not only with a framework but also with the tools to apply it so you can navigate the complexities of your business with ease, focus, and confidence.

— David Liddell
Boston, MA
2025

Introduction

In the pages that follow, I invite you on a journey that begins with a simple yearbook entry from my high school days—a declaration that, in hindsight, set the course for a lifetime of purpose and passion. Little did I know then, when I wrote "Consultant" as my answer to "Most Likely Profession," it would become not just a career speculation but a calling. Throughout my life, I have found unbridled joy in teaching, problem-solving, and pursuing entrepreneurial endeavors, and these qualities have woven the tapestry of my diverse career. My path has traversed through strategic organizational development, business expansion, sales, marketing, training, and the intricacies of industrial, engineering, manufacturing, technology, and electronic sectors. The first half of my career was a journey through various organizations, and each provided me with invaluable experiences that would eventually fuel my passion for starting my own consulting business and penning this book. However, among these pivotal experiences, one company stood out as a true catalyst.

I entered this organization as a regional manager tasked with overseeing all sales operations in the Northeastern United States. The company specialized in providing engineered heavy industrial equipment to the petrochemical industry. During my tenure, the industry was undergoing a period of consolidation, and our organization had just acquired another company. This merger required integrating two manufacturing facilities and implementing significant organizational restructuring.

What should have been a relatively streamlined process that lasted less than six months stretched out agonizingly for almost eighteen months. The consequences were profound, leading to major shipping delays and quality issues that left our customers extremely dissatisfied, ultimately resulting in lost business. Unsurprisingly, for most, the CEO was relieved of his position six months later.

In conversations with my closest colleagues, a multitude of issues emerged: equipment delays, inadequate coordination and communication, and a shortage of talent in critical roles, to name a few. However, at the core of the problem was the stark absence of effective leadership and an overwhelming sense of chaos that paralyzed both individuals and teams.

Reflecting on those days, I can confidently assert that "it just did not need to be that complicated," and with a better blueprint, they would have achieved their goals, and the CEO would have kept his job. Many businesses are inherently complex, yet they must incorporate a degree of simplicity and standardization in their operations to facilitate scalability, growth, and long-term success. It is imperative to maintain clarity regarding the business's mission, target audience, the products or services it offers, the value it delivers, and the most efficient methods for delivering that value. This principle became my guiding ethos for launching my business and forms the core essence of this book.

In 2001, I established Liddell Consulting Group LLC, a management consulting firm that offers strategic planning, advisory, training, and coaching services across diverse industries, primarily focusing on manufacturing, AEC (architecture, engineering, and construction management), and high technology sectors. For more than two decades, I have actively collaborated with organizations seeking direction and have provided one-on-one guidance to leaders aiming to inspire and foster connections within their teams. This journey has underscored the significance of fundamental and uncomplicated leadership principles, demonstrating their capacity to empower leaders and organizations to fulfill their objectives and nurture a resilient corporate culture.

The stories in this book, collected through my work with CEOs, business owners, senior management, and human resources executives, tell the collective tale that outstanding personal and organizational results within any business are merely being stifled by behavior and performance gaps. Continue reading, and you, too, can unearth and wield the necessary skills to transform your business into an efficient, innovative, and successful operation.

In a world teeming with business complexities and challenges, where leaders find themselves entangled in a web of conflicting goals and priorities, there is a pressing need for guidance that cuts through the noise and illuminates a clear path forward. This book is the beacon of light for those seeking to untangle their organizational maze and pave a way towards lasting success.

I have developed this book on the bedrock of my overarching success framework, which is meticulously designed to swiftly elevate leadership and business performance. This formula comprises three elemental components: Target, Energize, and Influence.

Part 1, Target, is about establishing a baseline for success. This section will explain that each business has its fundamentals, the difference between managing and leading, and how to create direction for your company.

Part 2, Energize, examines activating people, building consensus, and mobilizing teams. All of these components can be accomplished by fostering trust, motivation, and potential in your teams.

Part 3, Influence, finalizes mastering execution and delivering consistent results. This section will teach you how to connect people to value, measure success, and create accountability in order to establish effective and long-lasting change in any business.

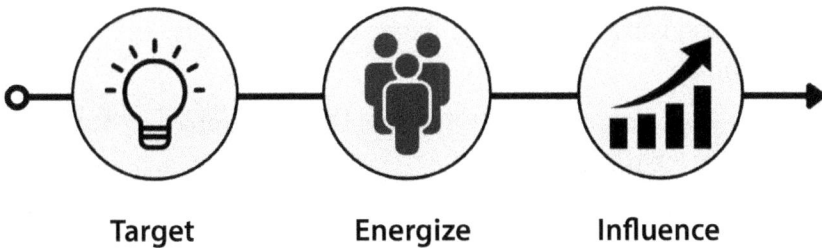

Target   **Energize**   **Influence**

Understanding and applying these elements will help you untangle the intricate web of business, resulting in a clear and practical path forward for you and your company to take confidently and competently.

My primary aim is to empower you, the reader, with unwavering confidence in your ability to translate the principles discussed in this book into actionable strategies applicable to your organization. I want to see you on a journey that leads you toward a newfound ability to strengthen your enterprise. The culmination of this journey will be a resounding toolset, an arsenal of strategies, and a renewed vigor to steer your businesses toward a pinnacle of success.

For countless leaders, their organizations often resemble difficult puzzles where goals, priorities, and obstacles intertwine without clear logic. This book offers a solution that unveils clarity from chaos, ushers in transparency, and charts a course forward that is both pragmatic and scalable, breathing new life into your business. Drawing from two decades of experience nurturing a diverse array of organizations and leaders, I am excited to present an engaging guide that will hopefully teach you something new and useful. I present to you a blueprint, a map that navigates the tumultuous waters of modern business leadership with wisdom and poise. This guide leaves you with not only profound insights but also tangible tools and a comprehensive roadmap to action. In these pages, I lay the foundation for you to unlock the dormant potential within your organization and turn aspirations into actions.

As you immerse yourself in the chapters that follow, you will embark on a transformative journey guided by principles that will help you to:

- Construct a roadmap leading to heightened performance and enduring business triumph.
- Discern the wheat from the chaff within your business: amplifying the strengths and addressing the weaknesses.
- Equip yourself with a profound comprehension of how and when to wield the levers of performance.
- Catalyze seamless communication: uniting your organization under a common mission and inspiring unwavering commitment.
- Channel energy and resources with precision and efficacy: minimizing wastage and maximizing impact.
- Harness the innate potency of leadership to invigorate and empower the workforce.
- Illuminate the intricate pathways along which value courses through your organization to the ultimate beneficiary—the customer.
- Instill a culture of accountability through deliberate expectation-setting and adept employee coaching.

- Foster a leadership discipline that is resolute, effective, and devoid of abrasiveness.

The success framework at the heart of this book is the pivotal concept that crystallizes the essence of the journey you are about to undertake. It serves as the guiding star for leaders and organizations seeking enhanced performance, unrestrained growth, and a compass to navigate the tumultuous seas of sustained success. The root causes of organizational dilution—lack of focus, convoluted models, and inconsistent execution—are the very stones upon which this concept is founded.

I wrote this book because I want to share this knowledge. I want to empower you and help you along this journey, wherever you may be in the process. In the past two decades, the biggest lesson I have learned from working in this space is that consistency is key for you and your company to succeed. Although this takeaway seems simple and straightforward, it can be applied to almost anything you are striving for success in.

However, keep in mind that this isn't magic. This book explains that achieving goals isn't about tricks but about using existing practical tools. A map tells you the best route to take in order to arrive at your destination, and this book is no different. I hope to teach you how to set goals, lead effectively, and think logically. As a leader, it is your job to communicate clearly and ensure everyone is on the same page. So, together, let's learn how to generate success by applying practical tools and establishing a clear plan.

This model's approach to strategy and leadership isn't as complex as it might seem; in fact, it is designed with simplicity in mind. We all have blind spots, and it's worth acknowledging that there are unknown unknowns—things we aren't even aware of and are overlooking. This concept underscores the significance of embracing fresh viewpoints and gaining insights, essential for making sound decisions and achieving effective leadership.

Part I

Target

Establishing a Baseline for Success

Chapter 1, "Turbulent Waters," delves into the unnecessary complexities businesses face and strategies for identifying underlying problems.

Chapter 2, titled "Managing vs. Leading," emphasizes the differentiation between management and leadership, emphasizing the significance of achieving the ideal equilibrium for a productive work environment.

Chapter 3, "Creating Direction," underscores the necessity of leaders in establishing a clear path for their organizations and fostering employee engagement and focus to drive results.

CHAPTER 1:

Turbulent Waters

In mid to late 2019, I spoke at the University of New Hampshire's annual leadership and management conference. As soon as I had finished speaking, I was approached by a man who introduced himself as Dennis. He told me he really enjoyed my talk and wanted me to come in to consult with his organization. I was pleased, my talk had obviously hit the right points. He went on to explain that he was having difficulties working with his business partners and was also trying to resolve logistical issues within his firm. Dennis had certainly got my attention. We chatted for a while, discussing his firm's practices and his views on the role of a team leader.

I visited his graphic design firm about a week and a half later. Dennis grew up in a small town in California but moved to Boston about 20 years before our paths crossed. He originally joined a very prominent design firm out west but ended up branching out and starting his own firm with his business partner. They quickly became successful and brought in $10 to $12 million annually.

Nevertheless, upon visiting the team, I was almost immediately confronted with their challenges. The main problem was Dennis himself. His domineering personality caused a lot of tension between him and his business partners. Dennis wasn't a team player; he always wanted to be in charge.

My role was to advise Dennis's management team on leadership and development. Initially, though, he saw this work as something meant "for everyone else" and resisted engaging with it himself. Over time, however, our relationship shifted. I had a breakthrough, and Dennis began to see me as his personal coach. Once we redefined how we worked together, he started to truly listen and embrace the insights I shared for his personal growth and for the company's success.

The biggest challenge I encountered was the absence of a written strategy. Without it, even minor uncertainties quickly spiraled into widespread confusion. Dennis kept all his ideas locked away in his head—helpful only if his team had the ability to read minds. Determined to be in control of every inch of the business, he simply refused to share. Another problem was that the leadership and management team was very loosely defined. So loosely defined, in fact, that the organization chart he initially showed me had fifteen people reporting to him directly. This felt less like a team and more like a dictatorship. The chart he showed me merely represented the power structure as his mind would have it—it offered nothing on the day-to-day management of a multi-million-dollar business. It was easy to see why employees were resentful. Dennis's leadership style made them feel powerless and undervalued.

Dennis also kept the business's financials very close to his chest. This meant there was a lot of uncertainty within the wider organization. Covid-19 exacerbated this; the business took a hit but he failed to disclose much to his colleagues, who were left to worry in the dark. This was in part due to his abundant lack of trust in anyone. (I suppose I should be very humbled by the fact that he trusted me.) This lack of trust created such a significant rift in the business that it was palpable within the company culture as soon as I entered the office building. Since Dennis insisted on signing off on everything personally, the business itself was robbed of its autonomy, as even the smallest decision had to meet his approval before being passed, causing a huge drag on overall efficiency. He frequently demonstrated his power mania with remarks like, "None of you know how to run a business" and "I'm the only one who can run this business; you would all run this place to the ground." He was very quick to dismiss anyone else's capabilities and put no faith in their ability to learn. When someone showed interest in learning the ropes so they could contribute more to client projects, he'd claim that he did not have the time to teach them and that it was simply easier and faster to do the work himself. As history has taught us, dictatorships rarely end well.

As a result of this toxic culture, people were drained of any motivation, other than to show up and collect a paycheck. His team members had no vested interest in the business because they were robbed of the ability to influence and inspire. I also noticed that everyone who worked there was at least 15 years younger than Dennis—this may have been part of his hiring strategy, as it seemed that he wanted employees to be young, dumb, and obedient. He was able to flaunt the argument that "with age comes wisdom", which was his solution to crushing any dissenting voice or sign of personal ambition. Of course, the reality was that these young employees were desperate to develop their skills to make the best of their careers, and they resented Dennis for preventing this. This business was simply impossible to scale, so long as he continued to withhold information as gatekeeper over a disempowered management team. Selling the business would have been impossible, too—who would want to buy a business that kept all of its internal planning and financial data in the confines of one man's brain? The lack of shared consensus meant that everyone in a leadership position was working in a different way—simply put, their business processes were nothing short of chaotic.

Graphic design is about creativity, sharing ideas, and teamwork. Early on during the Covid-19 pandemic, Dennis was flatly against working from home. However, remote working was sometimes inevitable, which caused him considerable distress. He only had himself to blame; had he offered employees greater autonomy and trusted more, the transition to remote working would have been far less stressful. As a result of the rigid, top-down business structure, they struggled during this global crisis. They hired 18 people that year, but by the end of the year, they had 18 jump ship. The attrition was made up of mostly senior/mid-level employees who felt their positions had become impossible to manage. The instability within their human resource pool made the idea of a succession plan even more out of reach.

Despite Dennis's organizational challenges, he had built a strong reputation in the business world and managed to retain several key clients. My mentorship and consultation helped the company avoid a significant meltdown, but the journey to this point had been long and fraught with obstacles. Since our first meeting in 2019, I have introduced many of my strategies into the business. While some gained traction, others struggled to break through Dennis's entrenched mindset.

One of our initial steps was bringing together the company's key thought leaders. Each participant was encouraged to share ideas—big or small—on ways to improve the business. I also guided this group through an intensive leadership development program, which laid the groundwork for tightening their management structure. While it was just a starting point, it was essential to addressing their foundational challenges.

But Dennis's poor relationship with his leadership team was the elephant in the room. It was time for something more intensive. I wanted to clear the air, get individuals to open up, and learn to be more collaborative. So, I decided to hold a series of leadership summit meetings, which offered team members an opportunity to discuss their goals, strategies and challenges, hoping to strengthen their business relationships. The attendees participated in presentations, workshops and roundtable discussions. On top of that, we also developed a mentorship program, and since the organization was highly matrixed, it was due for a makeover. Essentially, no one knew who their boss was. As a result of all our hard work, the company operates under much clearer guidance and has a development plan that is shared throughout the organization. Adding some structure to business operations paved the way for greater trust and better working relationships.

What Happened?

You might be wondering how a successful business found itself in such a mess. It's not as if the team leaders suddenly woke up one day to discover they had a major problem on their hands. Challenges like this rarely appear overnight—they build up gradually, much like cracks forming in the foundation of a house. At first, the signs may seem minor, even insignificant—a small fissure here, a slight shift there. But if ignored, those cracks spread and deepen until the entire structure is at risk of collapse.

Unfortunately for this business, those early warning signs went unnoticed. A lack of communication between leadership meant the issues grew unchecked, turning what could have been a simple repair into a costly and complex restoration effort.

In the remainder of this chapter, as well as in chapters 2 and 3, we will explore the first part of the success framework, *Target—Establishing a Baseline for Success*, which was outlined in the introduction.

A key ingredient of this baseline is understanding your issues. If you allow underlying issues to stagnate within bad practices, they will eventually escalate into "make or break" situations for your business. By failing to take immediate action, you risk turning your business into a complicated web of problems, inconsistencies, and failed efforts. However, if these issues are recognized and addressed early on, you will allow yourself the opportunity to build a stronger organization with a tougher and more seamless structure. Here are a few common problem areas I encounter regularly:

Poor Communication

How hard can this be? There's nothing simpler than a face-to-face conversation, where questions are raised and solutions are offered, right? Well, in a business context, communication can be a little more complicated than that. With hierarchies, different layers of decision-making, individual and collective authority, and, of course, egos, the process of communication can quickly become challenging. With a large organization, not everything can be casually talked out over at the water cooler or over a coffee in the break-out room. Departments will need to get together and sign off on their area of expertise; so, to facilitate good communication, you need cooperation and collaboration. Good communication is essential for a sustainable and healthy business relationship between colleagues at any level of the leadership hierarchy. The secret to good communication is ensuring the message delivered is the same as the message received. Communication isn't simply about relaying information; it requires listening, discussion, and confirmation of understanding. Here's a good rule of thumb: you have one mouth and two ears, so listen twice as much as you talk. Invest a little extra time to ensure intentions and meanings are understood—this will save you a hell of a lot of time down the line.

Ambiguity in setting expectations

In high-performing businesses, company goals and objectives are established by senior management and then skillfully cascaded down through the organization. Information transcends, level by level so that each department, team, and employee knows exactly what is expected of them and how they can measure their own success. Unfortunately, this is sometimes easier said than done. Managers are often better at defining people's day-to-day job descriptions than they are at determining the specific parameters that quantify a team or individual's success. For example, common business jargon like "hit your goals," "give 110%," and "gain traction" doesn't mean anything without the context of an associated task or overall goal that needs to be completed. Being told to "do better" or even "be the best" is worthless if you don't know what this looks like on a practical level. Leaders need to set clear and achievable parameters if they expect to see specific results. This also involves sharing relevant details with your team so they know how to quantify their success and build upon their failures. So, do the opposite of what Dennis did!

This ambiguity can manifest itself in multiple ways. Some businesses, like Dennis's, simply don't have a plan in place, leaving the organization with no sense of direction. Others have a plan in place but aren't fully taking advantage of a critical component of it. Sometimes, this is because the neglected area is complex and needs more time and effort dedicated to it. Other times, it's because the organization is pushing for something that is impossible, so you need to reset their coordinates and work toward more appropriate goals. Dennis's problem was that he made a lot of assumptions about what people knew and what they didn't. When he got upset about someone underperforming, he assumed they knew the baseline for performance—although they'd had to have read his mind for this to be possible! Dennis's biggest issue was leading people; he understood the raw mechanics of his business but did not know how to breathe life into that structure.

Lack of Accountability

A strong culture of accountability is essential to fostering openness and honesty within your business. This starts with leadership, as accountability thrives when those in positions of power set the tone by leading through their actions. Leaders must be willing to address issues head-on, even when difficult, as avoiding confrontation only weakens the organization's foundation. If a manager allows fear of conflict to overshadow the need for discipline or course correction, it sets a precedent for the rest of the team to do the same.

Accountability is not about finger-pointing or fostering a culture of blame. Instead, it's about creating clarity and setting clear guidelines and expectations so everyone understands their roles and responsibilities. When leadership models accountability, employees are more likely to adopt best practices, work with integrity, and maintain a high-performance standard.

Ultimately, accountability serves as a shared compass for the organization. It aligns individual and team efforts, ensuring that everyone works toward common goals with purpose and responsibility. Without it, even personal accountability becomes difficult, leaving individuals and teams adrift.

Conflict Avoidance

Those in managerial positions cannot bury their heads in the sand to avoid conflict. When a team or individual employee makes mistakes, this needs to be addressed head-on. Whether it be direct disobedience or misunderstanding, the cause of poor performance needs to be identified, and a resolution offered at the first possible opportunity. This isn't always easy as it is natural (for most people) to want to avoid conflict. However, harmony is not always found by protecting the status quo. If changes need to be made, don't delay; this will only leave you with a more challenging problem if things escalate. Once again, those in charge need to lead by example, as a healthy culture of open discussion requires a model that reaches from the very top to the very bottom. Often, passive managers who avoid conflict will eventually find themselves in a situation far worse than they were originally side-stepping—with explosive repercussions. Failure to deal with little problems will only breed big ones. It is also not fair on employees; if you are not honest with them from the start, they are denied the opportunity to mend their ways before the consequences become too grave. So, anything short of straightforward feedback is letting everyone down, nobody wins here, the employee is not learning, and the manager is left frustrated by underperformance. With the right mindset and leadership skills, "conflict" can be a powerful tool that opens minds, enhances problem-solving, and provides business innovation.

Complacency

An easy pathway to failure is routed through complacency. Sometimes, a business is most vulnerable when the economy is booming, performance is improving, and business is thriving. The fact is, no leader is immune to this, it is all too easy to be complacent when the going is good. However, this can be avoided if we consistently remind ourselves that a little caution is healthy. If we are too emboldened by our own success, we are in danger of adopting a superiority complex that makes us feel invincible. It only takes a few reckless decisions, made with too much confidence and not enough caution, to make the whole business crumble. For every good day you are enjoying now, remember there will be fewer good days or bad days to come. Complacency can demotivate employees, who no longer feel challenged. Over time, this will transform itself into poor productivity, fewer new ideas to drive competitive differentiation, and ultimately reduced profitability. And there you have success breeding failure, which, with a few simple safeguards, could have easily been avoided.

You need to continuously monitor your organization's performance and identify potential areas for complacency. Complacency can be proactively combatted by promoting a culture of innovation and encouraging employees to creatively and consistently challenge the status quo.

Poor Process and Shortcuts

With just a little determination, good employees will overcome poor process; however, this isn't the mentality you should rely on. For most organizations, it is wired into the company's DNA to always work towards maximum customer satisfaction. However, while this is good for customers and company profitability, this can place undue pressure on the employees doing the work. Often organizational processes are not even written down and are simply based on "the way we've always done it." This is adequate for very small businesses but won't provide the foundation for scalability and continuous improvement—a must for companies trying to expand and grow. Poor processes and shortcuts will lead to inefficiencies in the way work is completed, resulting in wasted time and energy. The business will likely suffer from decreased productivity, quality issues and increased business risk. Employees risk experiencing decreased satisfaction in their jobs, as they may feel that their work is not being valued or that they are not given the tools they need to succeed. In order to mitigate these risks, leaders need to make sure that effective processes are in place, and that employees are properly trained and have the necessary tools to follow them. Furthermore, leaders should continuously evaluate these processes and adjust as needed to improve efficiency, reduce risks, and increase flexibility.

Recognizing Key Signs of Organizational Stress

It is probably not hard to discern if your organization is stressed or facing issues that can present in many ways. However, determining the cause of stress is much more challenging, and there is never a one-size-fits-all solution. Just as a runny nose could be the first warning sign of an oncoming cold, the symptom can be traced back to a myriad of root causes. To truly determine the cause of any stress within an organization, a careful analysis of the people, processes, systems, and technology is required to understand how they interact with each other and if any underlying issues may be causing performance problems or dissatisfaction.

Consider these important business drivers in your organization: (1) delivering value to your customer, (2) nurturing effective leadership and employee empowerment, (3) displaying highly efficient operations, and (4) achieving stable revenue growth and profitability. The most common signs of stress become evident when one or more of those drivers is underperforming. Organizations must ensure there is enough visibility and transparency for these issues to be addressed effectively before they become a major problem for the company.

Delivering value to your customer

Organizational stress due to customer satisfaction issues can be a real problem for any business, and when customers are unhappy, it can reflect poorly on the entire company. Worse, you lose your customers. Some telling signs to keep an eye out for include:

- **Decreasing profits:** A decline in profits may signal internal issues affecting customer satisfaction, such as poor service quality, unmet expectations, or operational inefficiencies.

- **Inefficiency or low productivity:** Struggles to deliver on commitments or follow through with customers can create bottlenecks and increase stress throughout the organization.

- **Employee dissatisfaction:** Disengaged or unhappy employees often point to deeper problems within the organization, such as inadequate support, unclear expectations, or a disconnect from customer service goals.

- **Rising customer complaints:** A surge in complaints often reflects a failure to effectively address customer concerns, suggesting gaps in service or responsiveness.

- **Late deliveries:** Frequent delays in delivering products or services can indicate process inefficiencies, resource constraints, or mounting organizational strain— all of which ultimately impact customer satisfaction.

If something internally is causing a decrease in customer service, these symptoms are often reliable indicators that something is amiss. To combat these issues, proactively assess your customer needs and respond appropriately. For example, you may want to investigate the root cause of customer complaints and address any underlying problems that may be causing them. This could include updating procedures, training staff on customer service techniques, or incentivizing customers to stay with the organization.

Nurturing effective leadership and employee empowerment
Of the multitude of contributing factors to organizational stress, several are related to the organization's internal culture and leadership capabilities. When strong, capable leadership is absent, employees often feel they aren't given the support they require to succeed, leading to low morale. Watch for these signs to determine if intervention is required:

- **High employee turnover:** A high rate of employee turnover can indicate organizational stress, as employees may be leaving the organization due to dissatisfaction or a lack of engagement.

- **Increased absenteeism:** An increase in the number of employees taking sick days or being absent from work can indicate organizational stress, as employees may be experiencing burnout or high levels of stress.

- **Low morale and motivation:** Low morale and motivation can indicate organizational stress as employees may be disengaged and demotivated due to high levels of stress or dissatisfaction with the organization.

- **High levels of conflict:** High levels of conflict within the organization can indicate organizational stress as employees may feel stressed and anxious due to conflicts with colleagues or management.

- **Reduced communication:** Reduced communication, or a lack of communication, is a sign that employees might be feeling isolated and disconnected, which can lead to stress and a lack of motivation.

Retaining top talent has become more important than ever, with the baby boomer generation retiring and leaving a significant gap in the industry's talent pool. Not only that, but post-COVID-19 pandemic, many employers report difficulty hiring and retaining enough employees to keep the wheels turning on the proverbial bus. With a lack of talented workers, your company must be more competitive than ever to attract and retain the best staff. This means that a positive employee experience is essential, as employees are now more demanding than ever when it comes to their workplace environment and conditions. If your company can't provide this, you risk losing out to competitors who offer employees a more supportive and engaging work environment.

Displaying highly efficient operations

Your company's internal operations are a critical lens for spotting and understanding organizational stress. If your team is duplicating efforts or struggling to complete tasks efficiently, it's a clear signal that stress is in the mix. The value your company provides to your customers is achieved through collaborative and collective efforts in all functional areas of your organization. Having clearly written and efficient processes within each functional area is critical to preventing organizational stress while fostering cross-functional collaboration ensures alignment and seamless support across the company's value chain. When this is lacking or misaligned, signs of stress may emerge, such as:

- **Dwindling Teamwork:** Teamwork is essential in many scenarios to meet objectives and deadlines or share critical information. If teamwork breaks down, it can lead to severe organizational stress.

- **Mistakes:** Mistakes can occur requiring rework.

- **Lower Profitability:** When it comes to producing a service, lower profitability can be a sign of inefficiency and a lower gross margin or profit margin than desired.

- **Stress:** Inefficiencies will burn people out.

Much of this comes from leadership, which is the ability to inspire people to work and achieve together. Without an empowering leader, employees may feel unsupported in their roles and may not have a firm grasp on their responsibilities. Over time, this can compound stress and cause frustration to build up.

Achieving revenue growth and profitability
Financial performance issues are often one of the easiest signs of organizational stress to identify, affecting everything from employee morale to overall corporate strategy. Businesses that experience financial challenges often face intense internal pressures that can cause unintended consequences that can ripple throughout the company. Issues with financial performance can introduce symptoms of stress that may include:

- **Poor or slow decision-making:** Under financial pressure, leaders often delay or become short-sighted, resulting in decisions that will have an adverse longer-term impact.

- **Cutting corners:** Under pressure, leaders may cut corners to meet financial objectives but this could have a detrimental effect on the organization and its goals. Often, corners are cut to meet short-term objectives without considering long-term effects on the organization.

- **Lack of consensus:** Lower profits lead to fewer resources, requiring leaders to make difficult choices. This can force people to become inflexible to protect the team or department.

Where to start your performance enhancement journey

Most organizations are in a never-ending process of self-improvement, typically resulting in a never-ending list of improvement priorities. It's a fair assumption that there is always something to fix in an organization but recognizing this fact is often easier than identifying the correct solution or remedy. Within the management ranks, there is often too much siloed thinking. Consequently, this limits effective root cause analysis and leads to only partial fixes or deferred responsibility. The intent may be all well and good, but intentions alone don't produce desired outcomes. Truly effective leaders are always looking forward and planning for the future, with an approach that is well-coordinated with their peers. Their plans may evolve along the way, but they always have a destination in mind, guided by the company's vision, goals, and objectives. It serves as a beacon in shaping decision-making, identifying issues, applying solutions, and informing shifts in strategic priorities.

Improving and growing your business involves identifying opportunities, planning to improve, implementing changes, and reviewing progress as a leadership team. As an organization, this can be done as often as desired, but typically, once, maybe twice a year is the best approach. You need to understand how your company is performing today in relation to where you want to be (typically 12 to 18 months in the future). The gap between the two is where improvements need to be made. Ideally, the leadership team performs this assessment, although it can involve others.

Three simple questions should guide the assessment. As a company:

1. What level of success do we want to achieve?

2. What operating norms will help us achieve our success?

3. What needs to change or be improved to achieve the success we desire?

However, this three-step model should not be considered a replacement for strategic business planning. This model assumes that your strategic direction has been defined and communicated, and this assessment acts to understand your progress and identify course correction as needed. However, if your organization does not have a clear plan outlining your longer-term strategy (typically 3-5 years), this approach will still provide value and insight—but working on a longer-term strategy should also be a priority.

What level of success do you want to achieve?

Success metrics define achievement and are a foundation block for all businesses. They are measurable data, commonly referred to as key performance indicators (KPIs), that provide valuable feedback to people, teams, and the organization as a whole, regarding performance levels within the business. Day-to-day metrics are usually viewed as leading success indicators (output measures like effort and actions) that help determine if current performance will lead to future success based on the quantity of work performed. Lagging success indicators (outcome measures) provide proof of past performance. For example, a manufacturing company will measure cycle time in their production process as an *output measure* that will help them predict their ability to achieve their profitability and on-time shipping goals as *outcome measures*.

KPIs should be defined and measured in four areas of achievement, also known as the "balanced scorecard," first introduced in 1992 by David Norton and Robert Kaplan.

- **Customer Satisfaction:** How your customers judge you on such measures as quality, timeliness, performance, service, and cost (i.e., on-time delivery)

- **Organization Culture, Learning & Growth:** The attitudes and work habits of people (i.e., provide employees opportunities for professional development & growth)

- **Internal Business Process & Operations:** Adequacy and efficiency of internal processes, competencies, technologies, and systems (i.e., effective cross-functional collaboration)

- **Financial Performance:** Indicators of financial health like return on investment, profitability, and gross sales (i.e., steady year-of-year growth)

It is important to have a concise and representative list for each area (in most cases, I recommend 2-3 KPIs per area of achievement, and some organizations identify up to 5) so that, as the title implies, you achieve balance in measuring your business performance. Ignoring performance in one area will eventually lead to performance degradation in another area.

What do you need to do to be successful?
Establishing your success metrics (KPIs) is one thing. Building and gaining commitment from your leadership team in order to reach your goals is a whole other matter. Imagine you are setting out on a road trip: you can place an 'X' on the map, but there will be many ways to reach that destination. The key is selecting the best path that will allow you to arrive safely with the least number of pitstops, traffic jams and unwanted hitchhikers. The same applies in business and determining how to get there should be outlined through the same four areas of achievement as identified in the previous section (customer satisfaction,

organization culture/learning and growth, internal business process and operations, and financial performance).

Using this framework, the question to answer is: "what must occur in each area of achievement to ensure the future success of the organization?" The answers will become your Critical Success Factors (CSFs) in the form of key organizational behaviors and operating norms.

What must you start doing to make this happen?
Answering this third question is the most involved because it requires a discerning mind, patience, and the ability to effectively identify root cause issues. However, it will bring focus and prioritization to your improvement efforts. Consider the following approach:

Achieving Performance Improvement

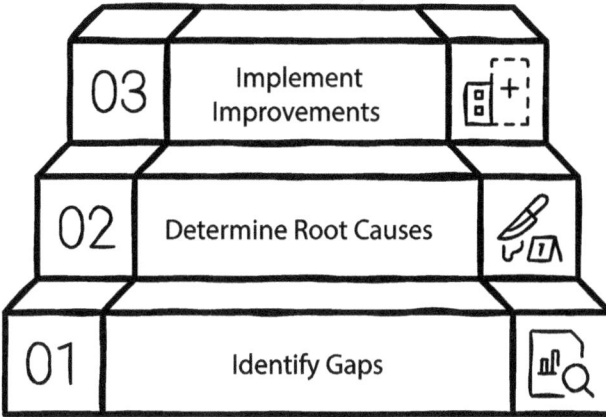

Performance gaps are calculated based on the difference between desired success (your KPIs and CSFs) and real performance. For example, an on-time shipment score of 78% would indicate a performance gap against a 95% target. The next step is understanding what is causing this gap, which requires a thoughtful analysis to identify root cause issues. Employing a fishbone diagram, force-field analysis, or pareto chart are examples of very useful root cause analysis tools. However, you don't have to get fancy, a roundtable brainstorming effort will get the job done as well. Select the best tool that matches your team's problem-solving style and personality.

Identifying and categorizing the root cause issues will tell you what to solve and will lead you directly to the improvement efforts that will fall into these five business elements.

Pathways to Success

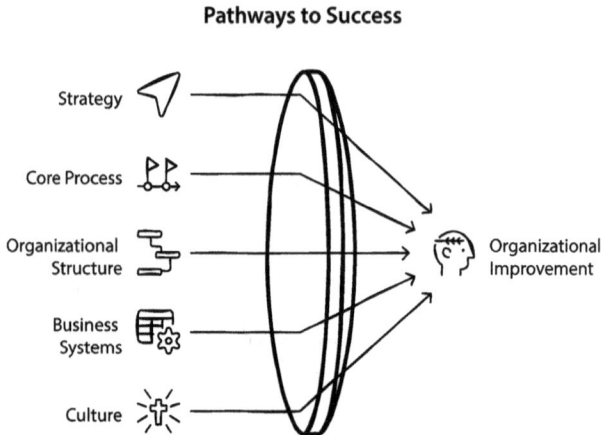

- **Strategy:** Identifies the direction and purpose of the organization, specifying products and services, market position, how the company differentiates itself from competitors, core competencies, and objective areas.

- **Core Process:** The major flow of work through an organization. Sometimes called the value chain when considering the entire organization, it is the sequence of events or steps performed by the organization to achieve its strategy and provide products and services to customers.

- **Organizational Structure:** Determines how people are organized around the core business process. It goes far beyond box charts, defining the boundaries between units, responsibilities, and relationships between people.

- **Business Systems:** Coordination systems, such as information sharing and communication, measurement and feedback, and policies and procedures, help employees develop within the organization. Development systems, such as recruitment and selection, training and development, and evaluation and feedback, help employees develop within the organization.

- **Culture:** How the organization operates based on leadership style, worker attitudes and habits, and management practices and beliefs that make up the distinctive "personality" of the organization.

In this process, it is likely you will end up with a comprehensive list of useful improvement ideas, actions, and projects. Prioritizing them will help you and your team focus your time and energy most effectively and will serve as a key tool for continuous improvement efforts.

The next chapter will dive into the key differences between managing and leading your teams. By now, I think you know which one I want you to focus on.

Key Takeaways & Actions Steps

1. **Communicate with Purpose for Understanding:** Effective communication within a team is essential to avoid misunderstandings and ensure everyone is on the same page. Leaders should prioritize open dialogue and active listening to foster a collaborative environment.

2. **Define Roles and Responsibilities:** Ambiguity in roles can lead to confusion and inefficiency. Clearly defining each team member's responsibilities helps streamline operations and enhances accountability.

3. **Trust and Empower Your Team:** Micromanagement and lack of trust can demotivate employees. Empowering team members by delegating tasks and trusting their abilities can lead to a more motivated and productive workforce.

4. **Establish a Written Strategy:** A documented strategy is vital to guide the organization through uncertainties. It provides a clear roadmap for decision-making and helps align the team's efforts toward common goals.

Simplicity Driven Leadership

CHAPTER 2:

Managing vs. Leading

Managing and leading people is a balancing act for any organization, and all managers in an organization must understand their differences, how they work together, and how to apply the appropriate mix for each situation. If this does not occur, the impact will be felt at every level of the company. It's important to understand that managing involves overseeing tasks and processes to ensure efficiency, while leading entails inspiring and guiding others towards a shared vision. To illustrate the difference between managing and leading, I'm going to start by sharing a real-life case study with you:

Mike and Amy own a 10-year-old high-tech company in southern Connecticut that provides managed technology services to businesses in the Northeast. In the first five years, they grew at a rapid pace, but that has declined to more of a modest pace. They are both smart people but exercise their talents through very different styles. As the VP of Engineering, Mike is very technically minded and likes to dig deep to understand the nuts and bolts of the technology and services they offer. He is task orientated—simply put, he likes to get the job done. Whereas, Amy, the company's President, has a high level of emotional intelligence, making her the natural leader in the organization.

While this partnership may sound compatible, the business has the potential to grow much faster. In order to improve and grow, they must identify their root cause challenges and where the friction exists, so they can meet their optimal growth potential.

In this case, the friction lies in the disconnect between their operating styles. They need to be more united in their approach to management and leadership. Mike has many years of experience in the industry; he knows what needs to be done and how—in this respect, he operates on the managerial side. However, he prioritizes resource management above and beyond any other aspect of the business, prioritizing "things" over people.

My mantra is: *Manage the business, and manage it well, but lead the people.* This means that people respond far better to being led rather than managed, which is where Mike falls short. Mike prefers to focus on cost reductions, operations, management, and streamlining efficiencies. While these areas are very important, he falsely believes that controlling these processes alone will drive success. Where he succeeds in managing, he fails in leadership.

This company is essentially run as the sum of two halves. Mike runs the technical and operational side of things, while Amy runs the sales, marketing and client-facing stuff, focusing on tasks that play to their individual strengths. This works up to a point. However, to operate a business successfully, you need to know how to bring in customers and inspire the teams you lead. Mike struggles with this as he likes to take control and is reluctant to delegate, a trait that is particularly challenging to overcome as a senior executive aiming to evolve from a manager to an inspiring leader. A good leader, on the other hand, will share responsibilities and empower teams to act autonomously in their area of expertise.

I coached Mike a few years ago in an attempt to teach him good leadership qualities and reach greater potential, but he was firmly set in his ways, driven by his tactical approach to management, which had him controlling every action from above. Mike only allowed me to work with him on a surface level, which meant not much would stick. By insisting that he is the ultimate decision maker over anything that is actionable, he is hindering the performances of those working underneath him. Like an English monarch wielding their privy seal, *Mike must sign everything off.*

This is an unfortunate case of micro-managing, or, as some people in his office quietly commented to me about his style, "Mike-romanaging." Unfortunately, Mike believes that the slow and modest growth the business *is* experiencing has little to do with his iron grip on operations; however, this approach is suppressing the rate at which the business can grow because his employees feel powerless and uninspired.

On the other side of the coin is Amy, who is far more strategic than Mike. She has a great success rate at bringing in business. Then it's Mike's responsibility to deliver on this business, and this is where the process starts to bottleneck as Mike-romanagement is stifling productivity flow.

Amy is the more natural leader. She knows how to talk to people and that the key to success lies in engaging and inspiring the people around her, ensuring they feel connected to the business. Amy understands that people are more productive when they are treated as more than "just employees," which can be achieved through a culture of creativity and innovation. She recognizes that the price of innovation is risk, as when investing in the creative freedom of her employees, you have to allow for mistakes to be made that are beyond your immediate control. Therefore, just as Amy delegates power in one half of the business, Mike is taking it away in the other.

Mike's risk-adversity causes him to hoard power. He isn't willing to delegate and he is overly-intolerant of mistakes. Ironically, his inability to trust causes as many mistakes as it prevents, as he is failing to teach and engage with those working under him. Conversely, Amy is driving the vision and empowering her team. She inspires people to be more engaged and motivated, allowing them the freedom to take on their own initiatives and make more decisions. I recall a specific situation concerning one of her salespeople and a sales presentation for a high-profile prospect that had the potential for a multi-million-dollar contract. Against Mike's wishes, Amy decided to delegate the entire responsibility to one of her up-and-coming sales representatives as a teaching moment and an opportunity to increase engagement with her team. This decision did come with some risk, but she felt it was the right decision, and she was proven right. They won the contract as one of their top ten in their overall history.

To look at this another way, Amy is offering employees the opportunity to succeed (glass half full), whereas Mike is anticipating his employees will fail, therefore doing everything himself (glass half-empty). By denying his team opportunities (the freedom to try, maybe fail, and try again), he himself has become the friction in his organization. So, here we have two individuals, both incredibly talented in the world of technology, yet what distinguishes them is their ability, or lack of it, to strike the right balance between managing and leading given the opportunity.

I have tried to teach Mike that getting people to perform well is not as simple as pushing them to "get things done." Instead, it involves helping people understand what success looks like through implementing goals, objectives, and KPIs. After all, every action or task completed is a means to an end. The employees involved in delivering those actions and performing those tasks should be empowered with the knowledge of what that end is, whether that be satisfying a customer or improving business performance.

I keep telling Mike the same thing, "Set your employees free!" To be fair to him, it's not that he isn't trying, but he is battling against his own reluctance to give up any control. Mike thinks he's offering a positive, supportive vibe, when in reality, he hovers over people like a hawk as they exercise any morsel of freedom he's handed out. It's like giving a kid a set of paints and telling him to have fun and express himself, only to loom over them, growling, "You're making a mess!" It's not that Mike completely flips out over every mistake, but he certainly tenses up and steps in too quickly with a critique and corrective action, which discourages innovation amongst his team.

Unsurprisingly, a frostiness has developed between Amy and Mike; they're like an old married couple, whose memories of the honeymoon are dead and buried. She is frustrated by Mike's inflexibility, and he doesn't understand what she's on about. They previously worked in the IT department of a large Fintech company before coming together to branch out into the technology sector. Despite all the good intentions that brought them together in partnership, the relationship is fracturing and unless something (or someone) changes, the future of the business remains on thin ice.

The Underlying Issue

Mike's attitude won't change until he stops viewing people as objects. He is entirely tactical in his approach to business, as he focuses on managing "things"— the problem is people aren't things. Things are merely there to be moved and manipulated, like chess pieces. People need support, guidance and the freedom to flourish. Yet Mike remains blind to the potential of the people in front of him. Not just particular people, but people in general. They are but the pawns in his game, while he is the grandmaster looking for a checkmate.

Mike's all: "you do this, you do that, you do this." But he needs to be more: "This is what we need to achieve together as a team. These are our larger goals and this is how we can all work towards them."

Self-Reflection

Of course, this chapter isn't just for Mike, it's also speaking to you. So, ask yourself, are you in a position to recognize the challenges before you? Are you clear on the differences between managing and leading? Do you apply them in an effective way? Are you getting the results you desire? Do people see you as an inspiring leader or a controlling manager? Do you often find yourself frustrated with your employees' performance, or are they thriving based on your leadership? And if you have accepted your challenges, are you well equipped enough to face them head on? Let's explore the difference between managing and leading in more detail to help you answer these questions.

Managing is a kind of mechanical approach to first building and then driving a business's performance (Mike's sole focus), but in order to operate successfully, you have to lead the people who facilitate the delivery of this (this is where Amy comes in). You need to have a direction to lead people, but this isn't just about having a plan. It is about engaging people in the plan, so they understand it and are invested in it. That's why understanding the distinction between managing versus leading is essential to your performance enhancement journey. The former does not function well without the latter. In the case of Mike and Amy, there is a power imbalance, and essential leadership strategies are being pushed out.

The reality is: you need to be spending more time leading people than managing them. Imagine a team of architects constructing a grand cathedral: the project manager doesn't just oversee blueprints, but also fosters collaboration among craftsmen. Like the architect directing the vision while relying on skilled artisans, effective leadership centers on empowering individuals toward a shared purpose. Bearing this in mind, a business thrives like an architectural masterpiece, not a rigid blueprint. While blueprints can guide actions mechanically, a masterpiece thrives on each artisan's expertise, working harmoniously under the architect's guidance, each empowered to contribute their unique craftsmanship.

This isn't to undermine the significance of management. It provides the builders with a blueprint—a goal to achieve and a set of guidelines to maintain stability. The key lies in having the right checks and balances, which are currently missing in Mike and Amy's business. An imbalance can lead to instability, eventually causing the enterprise to falter.

The mechanics of an operation, the "checks and balances," require human interpretation. If all that interpretation rests in a single authority, you cannot expect your output to be efficient or effective. Therefore, good leadership is essential if you want to maximize growth. Your most creative and productive asset will also be your human capital.

Too often, companies are willing to spend millions upon millions of dollars on buildings, marketing, and equipment—all the "things" that you can see in a business. These same companies will then balk at having to spend $50K or $100k on training their employees, after splashing the cash on all the tangible things that give a physical presence to the business. In this, they are neglecting the fact that people add value to these "things." Without people, equipment will just sit in place collecting dust. Neglecting people and hiding behind your technical or infrastructural might is a losing strategy. Cost-cutting the employee experience will leave them disenfranchised, disconnected and under-productive. How often do you hear of a friend or peer who has jumped ship because they couldn't see eye-to-eye with their manager? No doubt, they were over-managed and under-led.

It's essential to find a balance between the two, managing and leading. Senior executives need to lead those lower down the chain by setting the direction, envisioning the future, and thinking about building a stronger, better, more prosperous business. If the folks at the top are spending too much of their time managing, the balance is off—when *leadership* is provided from the top down, the operation manages itself at the lower levels. Strike the right balance and the cathedral will be erected flawlessly. Entrusting management responsibility to those you lead is a real game changer.

And now to a story of a real-life game-changer. This client of mine had recently finalized the acquisition of their sixth family-owned business. Their strategy involved taking over these small-scale enterprises and seamlessly integrating them into their existing manufacturing company, specializing in the medical sector. Following the purchase of this enterprise based in North Carolina, a pivotal decision was made—to introduce a fresh perspective. They appointed Tom, an external candidate, as the new General Manager. Given my ongoing collaboration with the acquiring company, I took the opportunity to pay a visit to their latest facility and extend a friendly introduction to Tom.

After chatting with him for a bit, I quickly learned that the business my client had acquired had been run from the top-down, under the thumb of the husband-and-wife team that owned it. Much like Mike and Amy's business, no one could make any decisions besides these two at the top. As a result, the company's growth was poor, although they remained profitable. This was due to the total absence of leadership at the team level. Their success came from the efforts of one of the owners, who went out as the face of the company, brought in new business, and then directed it through their facility to make money. However, with their lack of strategy, they hit a plateau and knew they weren't going anywhere without an injection of capital, which is why they decided to sell the business to my clients.

With a better understanding of the company history, I asked Tom how it was going.

"Well, it's pretty rough in here. I've got to say. The people don't respect one another. There's very little trust." But Tom was not going to roll over and be defeated; he estimated it would take him about a year to break away from this old culture and build the steps to better growth. "I'll need your help with some leadership development and team development work, David." I was more than happy to oblige.

"I need to get this team to start trusting each other so that they can work together to overcome some of the *real* challenges," he said. "They have serious business concerns, but they aren't addressing them because they don't know how to communicate with one another. We need to focus more on our direction, strategy, and what we need to achieve."

In his role as a turn-around expert, Tom made a notable commitment to a one-year assignment. However, his impact was nothing short of transformative within this seemingly short span. Not only did he manage to reverse the business's dwindling fortunes, but he also ushered in a new era of prosperity. A pivotal aspect of our collaborative strategy was the development of effective leadership, which served as a cornerstone for the company's future direction. An interesting pattern emerged as the dots began to connect: Tom's emphasis on leadership fostered an environment of trust within the organization. This, in turn, laid the groundwork for enhanced team performance and collaboration. And as the positive effects of this trust-propelled leadership rippled throughout the company, the results were remarkable.

Zooming ahead by two years, the company's trajectory had undergone a remarkable transformation. The revenue figures told a compelling story—a doubling in revenue, a clear testament to the efficacy of Tom's leadership philosophy. This evolution wasn't solely about numbers; it underscored a broader truth—that effective leadership, intertwined with trust, had become the bedrock on which the company's remarkable revival was built.

As Tom's one-year commitment ended, the company faced a critical juncture: finding a successor who could sustain the momentum and build upon the foundation Tom had created. Enter Nathan, the new General Manager, whose qualifications and leadership style were a perfect match for the company's longer-term vision.

When we sat down for our first meeting, I said, "Nathan, it's only been a little over a year, and you guys are on track to double your revenue."

"Yeah, it's amazing." He was clearly pleased with the lot he'd inherited. They hadn't employed more people; they didn't need to. They just removed the barriers and hurdles and empowered all the employees they already had. The most significant gains came from a fundamental shift in their leadership philosophy and associated behaviors. In the past, most managers believed that a top-down approach, where decisions were made at the highest levels and then cascaded through the hierarchy, was the only way to maintain control and ensure consistency. However, this rigid structure often stifled creativity and innovation at the frontline, where employees had valuable insights into customer preferences and operational efficiencies. Tom's transformative leadership philosophy challenged this traditional mindset by emphasizing decentralized decision-making and trusting employees to contribute meaningfully. Nathan continued this approach by fostering a culture where managers became facilitators rather than sole decision-makers. This cultural shift not only unleashed the untapped potential of their existing workforce but also solidified the notion that the true strength of the organization lay in the collective capabilities of its people. As a result, barriers were dismantled, and a new era of collaboration, agility, and continuous improvement emerged.

When we look at manufacturing as a business example, it becomes clear that driving revenue depends on several factors. First, you need the ability to attract and secure business. Then, you must effectively move that business through your facility, which is often constrained by the number of machines and the space available for them. If you run out of space, your options become costly—like investing in a new facility to expand operations.

But there's another way: an investment in people. Instead of adding physical space, this company focused on transforming a dysfunctional group of managers into a strategically minded leadership team. Developing their people unlocked untapped potential—no extra square footage required.

After conducting another team assessment, the progress was undeniable. The company had grown significantly, allowing for more flexibility in operations and breaking free from the restrictive dynamics of the family-led structure. Today, the leadership team works as a truly collaborative group, with every member focused on the entire business value chain.

The results speak for themselves—a thriving business driven by empowered people who make decisions with the bigger picture in mind.

As you think about your organization's potential, here are a few reminders about managing versus leading.

Leader Role

- Leaders must have a driving passion to realize their vision.

- Leaders build and sustain trust.

- Leaders are egoless and humble.

- Leaders inspire the commitment and motivation of their followers.

- Leaders are organizational and social architects.

- Leaders act from positive beliefs about people and situations.

Manager Role

- Plans and schedules work

- Directs resources to accomplish work

- Sets daily goals and priorities

- Measures progress

- Completes reports

- Runs meetings

- Maintains discipline

Key Takeaways & Action Steps

1. **Balance Management and Leadership:** Effective leadership requires a balance between managing tasks and leading people. While management oversees tasks and ensures efficiency, leadership involves inspiring and guiding others towards a shared vision.

2. **Foster a Collaborative Culture:** A collaborative environment where team members feel valued and respected enhances productivity and innovation. Leaders should encourage open communication and teamwork to build trust and improve overall performance.

3. **Adapt Leadership Styles:** Different situations require different leadership approaches. Leaders should be flexible and adapt their style to meet the needs of their team and the challenges they face, ensuring they can effectively guide their organization towards success.

4. **Recognize and Address Friction Points:** Identifying and addressing friction points between different management styles is crucial. Leaders should align their approaches to ensure a cohesive strategy that leverages the strengths of both management and leadership.

CHAPTER 3:

Creating Direction

When I think about helping my clients create direction in their business, I am always reminded of the satirical Randy Glasbergen cartoon of a CEO presenting a new mission statement to a senior manager containing just one word… "MORE."

"That's our new mission statement."

As ridiculous as this appears, it is more common than you think. I often encounter businesses with no written strategy at all. Worse, sometimes employees simply work from a set of arbitrary goals pushed down from the CEO's desk. One of my clients from a few years ago suffered from this phenomenon. They were a manufacturing company known for their cutting-edge products and innovative technologies, and they had always been a beacon of success in the industry. However, the company was about to face a challenge that would test its resilience and direction.

At the helm of the company was a charismatic and confident CEO named Allen. He believed in his instincts and had an uncanny ability to make strategic decisions on the fly. He considered written strategic plans to be bureaucratic hurdles that stifled creativity and agility. So, despite the recommendations of his leadership team and advisors, Allen rejected the notion of creating a formal strategic plan.

Initially, this decision seemed to align with the organization's culture of flexibility and rapid adaptation. Employees were empowered to act on their ideas without being bogged down by rigid procedures. The energy within the company was palpable, and employees felt a sense of freedom that was uncommon in corporate environments.

However, over time, cracks started to appear in the foundation. The lack of a clear strategic plan meant that each department operated in isolation, pursuing its own goals without alignment. The lack of a unified vision resulted in inefficiencies, duplicated efforts, and confusion among employees. Without a roadmap, employees began to question the direction of the company and their individual roles within it.

Over time, Allen's competitors began to gain ground. Their well-defined strategies allowed them to capture market share and establish strong brand identities. On the other hand, Allen's company found itself lagging behind, struggling to keep up with the changing industry landscape.

Morale among employees began to dwindle as the company's lack of direction became more evident. Without a clear plan, career growth seemed uncertain, leading to increased turnover and difficulty attracting top talent. The once-thriving culture of innovation started to wane as employees became disheartened by the lack of a collective purpose.

As financial results began to suffer, even Allen had to acknowledge that the rejection of a written strategic plan had been a mistake. The company had lost its competitive edge, and the impact was far-reaching—not only on the bottom line but also on the overall well-being of the employees.

In an effort to reverse the decline, Allen finally conceded to the need for a written strategic plan. It was a humbling moment for him, but it was a necessary step towards reinvigorating the company's fortunes. With the help of his leadership team and my guidance, a comprehensive strategic plan was developed, outlining clear goals, market analysis, and a roadmap for growth.

The transition was not easy, but the company slowly regained its footing. With a renewed sense of purpose and direction, employees found their motivation restored. Departments started collaborating, and the culture of innovation was rekindled.

Over time, the company transformed its setbacks into lessons learned. This experience highlighted the importance of striking a balance between agility and structure. The rejection of a written strategic plan was a cautionary tale, a reminder that even the most dynamic companies needed a roadmap to guide them towards sustainable success.

This is especially important for individual inspiration and motivation. Without a clear direction to guide your path, you'll inevitably find yourself lost in endless circles or meandering along at a sub-optimal pace. No amount of passion or zeal can make up for the lack of a legitimate pathway. Many will sacrifice a lot as a result of their dedication to their field; plenty are prepared to restyle their lives and uproot their families in pursuit of professional goals. However, too often, people will work tirelessly, in vain, focused on the wrong things.

Having a clearly outlined direction within a company creates a focal point for what needs to be achieved by individuals, leaders, teams, managers, and departments. It unites people at all levels of an organization, by focusing everyone on common goals and objectives. As the third critical piece in this part of the book about establishing a baseline for success, this chapter will explore how you, as a leader, can go about creating direction. You will need a strategy for creating direction, which is what we are going to dive into next. Because without a focused direction, your entire business will become hindered by ineffectiveness.

The Importance of Roadmaps

Once the organization has a clear direction, individuals will benefit from a more tailored approach to goal setting, which comes from a personalized "roadmap." Roadmaps provide individuals with a clear understanding of their role-based targets, which can be broken down quarterly, monthly or weekly, depending on the level of focus required. A general quarterly review may ask employees to collectively "focus on driving performance," for example, but this doesn't tell each individual the role they play in meeting this target. So, rather than staying at a high level, we need to look at the specifics—from the *what* to the *how*. This is where a roadmap can assist individuals in understanding what is expected of them, under the umbrella of the overarching company agenda. As a leader or supervisor, you want to make sure the roadmaps you provide aren't overly prescriptive, as individuals will always work best under the freedom of their own ingenuity. Instead, set guidelines or parameters to ensure focus, without tying anyone's hands behind their back. The alternative is a top-down, authoritarian structure, which I warned you about in the previous chapter when discussing the distinction between leading and managing.

Imagine you are given a continental United States roadmap and told to travel from A to B. You are free to travel whichever route you like, but you are told not to drive through the northern states, because the winters are too severe. Also, you must only drive on roads that are 65 mph or slower. So, you must remain in the south and your pace is limited—measures to keep you safe. Otherwise, the open road is yours to explore. This is an example of freedom with parameters. This approach anticipates and manages risk, whilst preserving a significant amount of freedom.

Freedom within a workspace is essential for individuals, teams, and departments alike. Any individual who feels they are backed into a corner with their hands tied, no matter their level of seniority, will start to resent the processes that govern them and those handing out the orders. This will breed a culture of apathy and demotivate and pacify the talent you have working for you. So, ensure any caveats within a road map are necessary, rather than needlessly prohibitive.

Whether it's with an individual, a team, or managing executives, there must be absolute clarity on what someone's responsibilities are and the degree of authority they are entrusted with. The key word here is "responsibilities", which need to be shared down the corporate ladder, rather than hoarded at the top. It's no good sharing responsibility if those then responsible are disinvested from the authority that facilitates it. Clarity is key. What you are looking for is an established timeline that spells out personal commitments. This allows teams or individuals to track their progress and empowers them with the knowledge of *how* they can contribute to company goals. Without this level of support in place, the responsibilities handed out become arbitrary, as those acting on them won't be able to prioritize their actions or deliver the change necessary to meet them.

It is a leader's responsibility to set people up for success. The fallout from the COVID-19 pandemic provides a clear example of what can go wrong when roadmaps aren't in place. With so many people sick or unable to work safely, the need for people to take on new responsibilities was more pressing than ever before. In many cases, this created a culture of confusion, where responsibility, authority, and the relationship between the two became unclear. It's like hiring a chef to prepare a meal, but when they arrive, they find that the kitchen is missing key ingredients and the necessary equipment. Sure, they know what dish you want and understand the end goal, but without the right tools and resources, they can't bring everything together to deliver the desired result. Back to Covid, people were stepping in, but had no idea where the lines were drawn; they weren't given bounds to play within, so they were left paralyzed by indecision— "I know what I could do but I don't know what I *should* do, or even if it's my place to try."

Often, a business will perform reasonably well without the roadmaps in place, but it only takes an unforeseen crisis to remind you why they should have always been there. At the height of the pandemic, businesses were losing millions and scratching their heads about the root cause. They lacked a clear understanding of roles and responsibilities, who was accountable for what, and the required business results.

Achievement Requires Ownership

Engaged employees are those employees who require less from you as a leader, as engagement is an extension of leadership. Employee engagement isn't something you can implement directly; it is the welcome side-effect of excellent leadership. This is implemented by all the things I have discussed already: setting direction, building trust, providing opportunities for growth and coaching. These are the leadership behaviors that foster a culture of engagement. But why is engagement meaningful? Well, when you have employees who feel they have ownership over what they do, they will almost always put in a higher level of effort, as they will feel more personally invested in their work as a reflection of who they are and what they do. By empowering your employees and nurturing their professional development, you'll benefit from a more productive work culture, reduce any risk of dissent amongst the ranks, and improve your workflow effectiveness as a whole.

The formula is simple and it works: engagement drives ownership, which drives accountability. Engagement necessitates accountability as goals are owned by a wider variety of stakeholders. This prevents you from finding yourself desperately fire-fighting a huge blaze from a high tower at the top. Making employees accountable presupposes their authority to fight their own fires—smaller fires are far easier to manage and far less likely to leave your company in structural ruins. If you build a culture where people feel, "I own this, this is mine," and "I want the results, I want to succeed as I'm accountable to this project, this team, and the company," your role as a leader will become far less stressful.

I recently spoke with a client who is a Divisional Vice President at an engineering company. He called me to discuss an issue he had encountered with one of his project managers (PMs) regarding a high-profile project they were engaged in. My client, we'll call him Joe, is slightly younger than his PM; at first, it seemed that the age difference was causing an awkward dynamic where the PM's life experience was at odds with Joe's seniority. Perhaps the PM felt like Joe was flaunting his power, or maybe Joe felt his PM didn't take him as seriously as the younger man. However, after talking with Joe for some time, I realized that age wasn't the underlying issue. He had two other PMs doing a fantastic job, so the other was an outlier, and he couldn't figure out why.

Joe continued to tell me more about the company, how the organization functioned before he joined a couple years ago, and some recent shifts within the business that may have caused confusion among the general employee ranks. I learned that the company was previously set up with all of the PMs (Project Managers) and PEs (Professional Engineers) in one big group without specific reporting lines of authority. PMs were assigned to incoming projects and requested engineering talent through a centralized coordinator to fulfill their technical needs.

Aside from the project delivery requirements, the structure was loose, and it lacked clarity regarding who reported to whom. Additionally, PMs and project team members were shielded from the financials of their projects, so few team members felt any sort of personal empowerment or accountability. After a little digging, I learned that the "Problem PM" was described as very good at delivering to customers and maintaining a very high quality when working on projects, but ultimately, his projects lost money.

Suddenly, it all made sense. I told Joe that I believed that the PM had felt disengaged under the old regime, as they were denied important information and the context that gave meaning to their role. None of this was his fault. He wasn't given the tools he needed to learn and grow. He was missing some of the critical skills required to be a good PM, which was evident in the way the business used to be structured. The good news was that things had changed. There was a hill for this PM to climb; he just needed to recognize the change and use the greater freedoms awarded to those in his position.

Success Measures

A key element to setting direction within your company is a set of performance measures that will define your success. This is required in all areas of your business, across all functions, and from the executive level down to the team and individual levels. The latter will allow your team members to assess their achievements within the context of overarching company goals.

Think of it like this: imagine you're climbing a mountain. At first, the goal is to reach the summit of a smaller hill, and once you get there, you feel a sense of accomplishment. But then, you look up and see a much taller peak in the distance. The view from your current summit now seems limited, and your goal shifts to conquering this new, higher mountain. With this new challenge in sight, your previous success takes on a different perspective, and your aspirations grow.

The higher mountain requires better equipment, more preparation, and a different mindset. Similarly, in the business world, leaders who set ambitious goals and provide their teams with the right tools to elevate their performance will drive the greatest success. As the challenges grow, so too must the strategies and resources needed to achieve them, ensuring continuous professional growth along the way.

Not only that, but this will also ensure that everyone is clear about what they can achieve if they exercise their full potential. This applies to employees or teams at every level—there is never a point at which you should stop encouraging personal growth. Employees will always offer the business more if they are continuously chasing the next biggest ascent.

Success measures are also referred to as key performance indicators (KPIs), and by definition (Wikipedia), they evaluate the success of an organization or of a particular activity such as projects, programs, processes, products, and other initiatives, to name a few examples of where they can be applied. There are two types of KPIs: *leading* versus *lagging* indicators. Your company should use both in order to improve and succeed over the long term. Leading indicators are basically the ways that we can measure a company's progress, improvement, and daily achievement. They are incremental in nature that, if achieved consistently, will lead to a company's eventual success; for example, a directive to bring in 50 new customers that each spend an average of $50,000 each over the course of the following calendar year. Lagging indicators provide similar value. However, they don't predict future success, they define success at the moment, looking back to see whether the intended result was achieved. Using the previous leading indicator example, an associated lagging indicator would have been $2.5 million in revenue in the calendar year. In the unfortunate event that the target is missed, an assessment of the performance against the leading indicators will provide a basis from which to improve, as well as making sure that the goals set are realistic.

Leading Indicators
An OUTPUT MEASURE that indicates the quantity of work performed in support of a goal (e.g., # of people served, # of transactions processed, # of permits issued, # of inspections conducted, # of proposals generated).
Lagging Indicators
An OUTCOME MEASURE which indicates if the work performed is making a difference by measuring what has changed in the world as a result (e.g., # of accidents, student test scores, revenue received, energy usage).

Companies that know how to measure *themselves against themselves*, month by month and year by year, will have a competitive advantage over those who do not. I have clients who are doing exceptionally well, and that is because they know precisely how well they're performing in all areas of their business using data strategically at an executive level, business unit level, team level, and individual level. By looking at this kind of data, they have a benchmark from which to measure their current success, which gives them a solid direction, focus, and ability to proactively self-correct.

Visualizations are incredibly helpful as well. The most successful companies will often use flat screen displays to share their results with all employees so they always know exactly how the company is performing at any given time. This helps people retain their focus, so they don't lose direction. To give an example of how important this is: I was meeting with a client who ran an aluminum extrusion business; essentially, they pushed hot aluminum billets through what looked like giant playdoh holes to reshape the metal into useful products. One of their primary KPIs (lagging indicator) was pounds of aluminum shipped per month. I was asked to work with the department leaders to help improve overall production performance, and we realized that the biggest bottleneck existed in the packaging and shipping department. Two teams in the department faced each other on either side of the shipping area, each with about four workers. I asked the department manager how they measure their daily success, and he explained that they weigh every shipment before it leaves the facility.

"Okay, but where can the workers see actual numbers and stats of their success that day?"

He walked me down a long hallway, about a 30-second walk from their work area. "Here," he said. It was a conference room with a TV screen mounted to the wall.

"This?" I asked. "But where is your proof of success visible from the workspace?" He quickly realized what I was getting at. About a week later, he had his IT team install a massive screen in the shipping department. It displayed a progression bar that went up bit by bit as they got closer and closer to their daily target. As a result of this simple solution, their output went up 2.5X within the first 14 days. Lesson learned: you need to give people a clear and accessible measuring device if you want to keep them motivated and goal-orientated.

Think of the trio of goals, objectives, and success measures like a waterfall. At the top, the main goals pour down into the next level, breaking into more specific objectives, and then cascading further into clear success measures at every level of the organization. Just like water flowing from one tier to the next, each part of the organization—from top executives to the frontline supervisor—receives their share of clarity and direction. Everyone can track their progress against measurable success, whether daily, monthly, or yearly. This cascading flow ensures that each individual's efforts are aligned with the broader goals, driving the entire business forward with clarity and purpose.

Key Takeaways & Action Steps

1. **Establish Clear Direction:** A well-defined strategic plan is essential for guiding the organization. Without it, departments may operate in isolation, leading to inefficiencies and confusion. A clear direction unites everyone towards common goals and objectives.

2. **Create Personalized Roadmaps:** Tailoring roadmaps to individuals' specific role-based targets helps them understand their specific targets. These roadmaps should offer guidelines without being overly prescriptive, allowing for freedom and creativity within set parameters.

3. **Foster Employee Engagement:** Engaged employees feel a sense of ownership and accountability for their work. This engagement drives higher levels of effort and productivity, as employees are more personally invested in their tasks and the success of the organization.

4. **Implement Success Measures:** Establishing key performance indicators (KPIs) at all organizational levels helps track progress and define success. Both leading and lagging indicators are important for measuring performance and ensuring continuous improvement.

Part II

Energize

Activating People, Building Consensus, and Mobilizing Teams

In Chapter 4, the focus is on "Creating Trust," delving into the crucial foundation of trust-building within the context of achieving success.

Chapter 5, titled "Creating Motivation," takes an in-depth look at the various factors and strategies involved in fostering motivation among individuals and teams.

Finally, Chapter 6, "Creating Potential," investigates the ways in which potential can be harnessed and maximized to drive the overall success process forward.

CHAPTER 4:

Creating Trust

I did some work early in my business with Hasbro, the toy company that produces Monopoly, originally created by Parker Brothers (purchased by Hasbro in 1991). I was referred to their manufacturing division located in East Longmeadow, Massachusetts, to work with the Vice President of Engineering. I was very eager to get started, especially after arriving at the old Milton Bradley (purchased by Hasbro in 1984) facility where, at the time, Monopoly was manufactured. It was an old building with many of its legacy games on display and Milton Bradley's original desk. Playing many of these games as a younger person was a real treat. The Vice President of Engineering, David, was an older guy, only a couple of years from retirement. I liked his style immediately and after meeting twice to discuss his objectives, he asked me to come in to do a leadership program for his team.

At the end of our second meeting, he wrapped up by saying, "This is what leadership looks like to me." He opened his drawer and pulled out a long piece of string. He laid it on his desk so that one end was pointed at him and one towards me. Long and straight. "Now, I want you to push on that," he instructed, motioning to my end of the string.

Puzzled, I pushed on the string and watched as it all bunched up into a pile of knots.

"Okay," the Vice President of Engineering said, "Now take that same end and pull it towards you. Then pull it anywhere you want to go on the desk."

I did as he asked, and the pile slowly untangled, and the string moved smoothly and freely across the desk, almost snake-like.

"That is leadership," he explained. "I want you to help my people to understand that leadership is like pulling on a string. You can't push people; you have to pull them with you. They have to want to follow you. They must trust you."

Trust is the lubricating oil that allows the engine of the business to run smoothly and efficiently. When you have it, you don't worry about it. But your engine will fall apart quickly when you don't have it. Trust is built one-to-one with individuals or small groups, but it can so easily be tainted. Trust can be elusive. You can go back throughout your life and think of one person who has your complete trust; now, ask yourself why you trust them. It might be hard to pinpoint exactly why, but that's okay; trust is a feeling you have. Every moment that has built up trust between you and another person is not written down in a spreadsheet, because that's not how trust works. Feelings towards someone can ebb and flow, especially in a work environment and so trust needs to be consistently worked on. Taking your eye off that trust ball will sneak up on you and bite you in the behind.

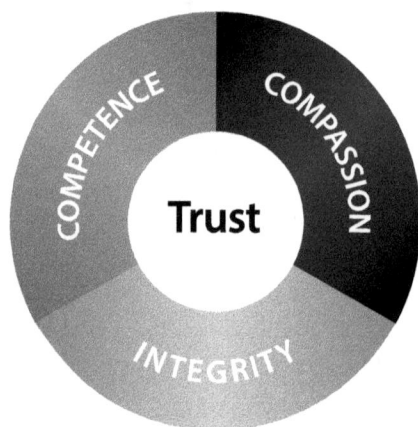

Trust stands as the bedrock of effective leadership, an intangible yet indispensable force that cements relationships, drives collaboration, and propels teams towards success. At its core, trust is a combination of three elemental pillars: integrity, competence, and compassion. *Integrity* forms a base where a leader's actions align with their words, fostering transparency and reliability. Honest and authentic leaders cultivate open communication, inspiring teams to tackle challenges collectively. A leader's proficiency and expertise instill confidence in their ability to navigate complexities and make informed decisions.

Competence, however, is not just about knowledge and skills; it involves a willingness to learn, adapt, and acknowledge limitations. A leader who humbly acknowledges what they don't know builds credibility, as their authenticity reinforces the trust others place in their capabilities. An empathetic leader who considers the emotions and well-being of their team members fosters a sense of belonging and camaraderie. *Compassion* involves active listening, understanding diverse perspectives, and showing genuine care for each individual's personal and professional growth. When leaders demonstrate compassion, they bridge the gap between authority and approachability, nurturing an environment where trust can thrive. Together, these elements create a balanced foundation. A leader excelling in one but lacking in others risks weakening trust. Mastery of integrity, competence, and compassion fosters an environment where trust thrives.

The spirit of a business, or any group, is usually based on the actions of a smaller subset, typically those in leadership or authority positions. As a leader, faith ultimately begins and ends with you. If you want to build solid and trusting relationships, you need to initiate them. Some people may be highly trusting of others and give people second or even third chances. Others are the opposite and say you have to earn that trust over a long period. If you meet someone and are having a hard time trusting them, you may naturally reserve your own trustworthiness. However, by withholding your trust, bias is the only development this dynamic creates between you and this person. The act of withholding trust in such situations can inadvertently give rise to a cycle of mistrust. Ineffectively withholding trust can confine the relationship within a cocoon of bias, preventing the potential for mutual understanding, meaningful connection, and collaborative growth between you and the other person.

Once that bias has been built, the only thing you see in that person is their untrustworthiness. Even if 99% of what they are doing is trustworthy, the only thing you are looking for is that 1% to reinforce that bias. Instead of maintaining and magnifying this destructive relationship, leaders can be liberal with their trust and see what comes back to them. Although trust can be elusive, and we don't know if people are trustworthy right away or not, by establishing yourself early on as a trustworthy leader, this destructive dynamic of festering bias can be avoided, and honest relationships between you and your people can begin to form.

A few years ago, I was working with a semiconductor company and was asked to help the leadership team build a stronger team function. My responsibility was to connect with the leadership team members, delve into the intricacies of their existing team dynamics, and ultimately facilitate the formation of a much stronger and more harmonious collaborative framework. Through a series of interactive workshops, one-on-one consultations, and strategic interventions, the goal was to unlock the team's full potential, fostering a cohesive environment where greater innovation and effective decision-making could flourish.

As the team started to embrace the process, I could see real progress taking shape. Communication improved, and collaboration began to feel more natural and productive. However, alongside this progress, it became clear that some individual dynamics needed more attention to fully unlock the team's potential. One such dynamic centered on Frank, a standout individual flagged by HR as someone who needed "extra help."

Frank led the Quality Group and was beyond tough on his people. When he reluctantly agreed to additional one-on-one coaching with me, it didn't take long to realize he was only going through the motions.

He was one of the most divisive managers I've ever encountered. Honestly, I hesitate to even call him a leader because he cared only about himself— being in full control and lining his own pockets. After talking to his team, I quickly confirmed just how severe his authoritarian approach was. He was curt, aggressive, and completely closed off. All information had to flow through him; he trusted no one, hoarded knowledge, and allowed almost no communication between the Quality Group and other departments. His team hated him for it, and the visceral distrust on all sides was impossible to miss.

The toxic dynamic within Frank's team was a textbook example of what happens when trust is absent. The lack of trust between Frank and his people had eroded communication, stifled collaboration, and created a culture of resentment and fear. It was clear that rebuilding trust would require more than just surface-level fixes; it demanded courageous conversations, a willingness to address conflict head-on, and a commitment to repairing relationships. This is the challenge—and the opportunity—of accessible trust. Once trust begins to take root, it becomes the foundation for navigating conflict, fostering open dialogue, and making mature, intentional decisions that strengthen the team and the business.

Once you open yourself up to accessible trust, taking action, engaging in necessary conversations, and making mature decisions become imperative to uphold that trust, particularly in moments of conflict. The inherent challenge with trust is its susceptibility to unintentional erosion, often triggered by seemingly innocuous actions like body language or an ill-fated remark. Yet these actions can lead to a corrosive atmosphere among colleagues and a detrimental business environment. While most individuals shy away from conflict and confrontation, building trust hinges on addressing such instances. Conveying discomfort within a relationship requires courage, yet it's essential for the mending process. Trusting in the potential for mutual progress is vital. Remarkably, conflicts, even when confidence is high, can be candid but non-personal, facilitated by the bedrock of trust. However, when trust is absent, conflicts devolve into personal confrontations, resulting in relationship breakdowns.

So, how is trust built? As mentioned earlier in this chapter, trust is built on three main pillars: integrity, competence, and compassion.

Let's start with compassion. Compassion for others begins with reminding yourself that people have different ways of doing things that may not be the same as yours. You need to listen to what they have to say and really take it in. If you realize you may disagree with them, it is still important to maintain respect for them. Compassion is the starting point for trust, the groundwork for which it is built. Once you have compassion for someone, it begins to not only develop your confidence in them but also instill their trust in you because they now know that you will still maintain the same level of respect and empathy for them, whether you agree or not.

Next is competence. Competence is all about how well you know what you're doing and how effectively you apply your expertise. It starts with your knowledge and experience in your industry—do you truly understand the nuances of your field? Are you skilled enough to navigate challenges and capitalize on opportunities? Equally important is your ability as a leader. Are you not only qualified but also continuously learning and growing to stay sharp and relevant? Competence also extends to your awareness and judgment—can you identify when someone on your team isn't meeting expectations or falling short of their goals? More importantly, do you know how to address those situations constructively to help your team and organization thrive? Being competent isn't just about what you know but how you use that knowledge to build trust, inspire confidence, and drive results.

And finally, integrity, which represents the guiding principles that drive you and your operation. Looking back at the financial crisis of 2008, we lost faith in many of our financial leaders because they lacked integrity. All the little guys lost their jobs, and the CEOs walked away with bonuses and millions of dollars. Where's the integrity there? Integrity doesn't require grandiose gestures—it's often reflected in the simplest actions, like showing up to meetings on time. If you're consistently late, consider the message you're sending. It signals a lack of respect for others and can be perceived as you believing you're more important or that your time holds greater value than theirs. Small actions like punctuality speak volumes about your character and how much you value those around you. Compassion, competence, and integrity form the melting pot of trust. You must remember, however, that there's a fine line between building trust and tearing it down.

Being a leader is all about how we communicate and the true connections we can make with others. Actively building relationships and establishing trust with your team members is one of the only ways to get them to willingly follow and take direction from you. You cannot come out of your hole, bark orders at people, and expect astounding results. That's not going to happen. People need human connection. They need to know that their energy and time are going to a place that values their efforts, a place where they are given room to grow if they fail. A common problem we see is a need for development in companies. So often, this is blamed on the laziness of the workers, and they are disconnected and unmotivated. Well, yes, one of those points is correct: people are disconnected, but, more often than not, this disconnect stems from the top.

The idea that "I am above you; therefore, I will not stoop down so low" creates an environment where workers constantly battle to do well but do not take enough risk to fail. If they fail or slightly miss the mark, they could get punished or, worse, lose their jobs. Trust is built on clear communication, which aims to make a connection and establish understanding.

In addition to conversation, body language, the non-verbal, makes up 50% of our communication with others. What you say and what you do need to reflect each other. I want you to be highly intentional with how you communicate with others, how you put your words together, the tone of your voice, etc. One of the easiest and most effective ways to establish trust through non-verbal communication is to actively listen. Many people in a position of power forget this. They forget that merely listening builds invaluable trust and levels the playing field, allowing workers to not only feel heard but seen and valued. A genuine and compassionate approach to communication encourages others and instills them with a sense of value and confidence.

In order to motivate the masses and energize a group, you need to be respected as a leader; and respect is built on trust. Workers don't *want* to show up to their job every day disconnected from those around them and uninspired by their projects, but oftentimes, they are symptoms of their environment. A Harvard Business Review article titled, "The Neuroscience of Trust," written by Paul J. Zak, states that establishing a "culture of trust" in a company can create a powerful impact on employee engagement and that, "employees in high-trust organizations are more productive, have more energy at work, collaborate better with their colleagues, and stay with their employers longer than workers at low-trust companies."[1]

But how do you foster this kind of atmosphere in your own company? Zak has found that eight management behaviors establish trust in your employees and that can reinforce the respect in a leader. By recognizing excellence, inducing "challenge stress," giving people discretion in how they do their work, enabling job crafting, sharing information broadly, intentionally building relationships, facilitating whole-person growth, and showing vulnerability,[2] a leader gives up micromanaging and enforces trust. Richard Fagerlin's book, *Trustology*, also delves into the importance of mutual respect and trust in the workplace. Fagerlin points out that trust and respect go hand in hand. Without respect, trust cannot

---

1   Paul J. Zak, "The Neuroscience of Trust," Harvard Business Review, January 1, 2017, https://hbr.org/2017/01/the-neuroscience-of-trust.

2   Ibid.

flourish, and without trust, respect is hard to sustain. He argues that organizations that prioritize both respect and trust create a culture where employees feel empowered, engaged, and motivated to contribute their best. This leads to increased innovation, stronger teamwork, and higher levels of job satisfaction.

"The first job of a leader—at work or home—is to inspire trust. It's to bring out the best in people by entrusting them with meaningful stewardships, and to create an environment where high-trust interaction inspires creativity and possibility."

— Stephen Covey

I've been working with a client for the last five years. Though he is making progress, he continues to struggle with trust to this day. He is the CEO of a successful manufacturing company in Massachusetts that has been in business for a little over twenty years. He started the business with his father and prides himself on hard work and attention to detail, likely a family trait.

Early on, I discovered that he had some misguided mistrust of his senior managers, which drove him to tightly guard financial information out of concern for potential mismanagement or errors. What he failed to realize, however, was that his team genuinely respected him, valued the company, and was eager to work together for its success. His inadvertent actions fostered a pervasive lack of confidence within his leadership team. In the years that followed, he has made strides in overcoming these tendencies, leaning towards healthy paranoia more than distrust. Yet, his most significant challenge remained: a reluctance to delegate authority and share information. He instinctually clung to control, impeding progress. As a result, his secretive approach left managers without essential context, inhibiting their decision-making, and ultimately slowing business growth.

About 18 months ago, two of his best managers became so frustrated that they quit, leaving the organization in a tenuous situation with a gaping hole in the leadership structure. This was the needed catalyst to allow change to occur. Now, five years into our journey, the CEO is truly stepping back and allowing his managers to step up. By demonstrating trust and acknowledging their fidelity to the company, he's starting to foster confidence in them. Though there's still room for improvement, the trajectory is positive. When leading with trust, remember that having faith in your team reflects self-assuredness. After all, you selected them for their roles—why not provide the opportunity for them to prove their capabilities? Forcing them into restrictive roles while expecting results of an unbound individual is impractical.

Key Takeaways & Action Steps

1. **Clarify Your Communication Intentions:** Always start with a clear understanding of what you want to achieve through your communication. Define your purpose and desired outcomes before engaging with others.

2. **Adapt Your Style to Your Audience:** Recognize the diverse communication styles within your team and adjust your approach accordingly to ensure your message is understood and well-received.

3. **Foster Open Dialogue:** Encourage an environment where open communication is welcomed and practiced. Actively listen to feedback and respond thoughtfully to build trust and mutual respect.

4. **Continuously Improve Communication Skills:** Regularly assess and refine your communication techniques. Seek feedback from others and be open to adapting your style to enhance effectiveness.

CHAPTER 5:

Creating Motivation

Let me share a story that highlights the transformative power of leadership within a high-tech firm on the cutting edge of its industry. Despite their cutting edge technology, the company was stuck in a rut. The workforce was uninspired, innovation had slowed to a crawl, and productivity was far below what it could have been. Employees were just counting the minutes until the end of the day, brainstorming sessions had turned into top-down lectures, and ideas were chosen for being "good enough" rather than truly exciting. Recognizing that things couldn't continue this way, the leadership made a bold decision to shake things up and create meaningful change.

That's when I was brought in to assess the situation. It didn't take long to see that the root of the problem was leadership—or rather, a lack of effective leadership fundamentals. Leaders were unclear in their direction, and decisions felt inconsistent and arbitrary. With no clear guidance, the organization's efforts were scattered, leading to missed goals and frustrated customers. Mistakes were ignored, employee morale hit rock bottom, and the entire workplace felt on edge. The solution? A leadership transformation program designed to realign the organization, reinvigorate the team, and rebuild a sense of purpose. The program focused on clarifying values, improving communication, and empowering employees to take ownership and drive change.

The visionary CEO, Emma, led this transformation. She wholeheartedly embraced my recommendations and set out to revamp the company's mission and values. Her goal was to ensure that these guiding principles resonated deeply with every member of the workforce. Furthermore, Emma wanted comprehensive leadership training, with a strong emphasis on empathy and collaboration. The outcome was truly impressive.

Managers, under Emma's leadership, began to listen more attentively to their teams and actively fostered an environment conducive to innovation. They implemented regular feedback sessions, encouraging open dialogue and empowering employees to voice their opinions. Emma also introduced a mentorship program, pairing seasoned leaders with promising talent and fostering a culture of continuous learning and development. This shift in approach not only boosted employee morale but also led to a surge in productivity. The impact of these changes was nothing short of staggering. A newfound sense of motivation swept through the workforce, translating into a wave of remarkable breakthroughs. With their renewed energy and determination, the company successfully launched three groundbreaking products, securing a significant share of the market.

This story underscores a powerful truth: visionary leadership has the potential to unlock the hidden reservoirs of passion, creativity, and dedication within employees, fostering a culture of continuous growth, innovation, and shared success. Leaders and company cultures that motivate their teams not only see better results, but more engaged workforces as well.

The Power of Authentic Motivation

Before we go any further, there's something I need to address—something that might seem obvious but is often overlooked. You cannot force someone to be motivated. When I hear leaders talk about "motivating their team" or "motivating an employee," I can already sense the uphill battle they're about to face. Motivation doesn't come from tricks or manipulation, and employees aren't machines you can program. They're people—individuals with needs, goals, and aspirations, just like you.

From a broader perspective, we all share a common truth: motivation thrives in the right environment. And it's up to leaders to create that environment. Leaders who demand exceptional results but fail to provide space for their people to grow, contribute, and thrive are setting themselves—and their teams—up for disappointment. True motivation isn't forced; it's cultivated through trust, support, and meaningful opportunities to succeed.

As a leader, it's essential to be open and willing to build genuine, one-on-one relationships with your team members. Doing so creates an environment where they feel comfortable reaching out to you when issues arise. By fostering open and honest dialogue, you make it easier for employees to bring concerns to your attention without fear of criticism or judgment.

Beyond keeping the lines of communication open, a great leader actively values and acknowledges the contributions of each individual. Sometimes, even the simplest gestures—a heartfelt "Thank you" or "This is great"—can make a tremendous impact. Recognizing hard work in meaningful ways not only shows appreciation but also strengthens the bond between you and your team.

Each individual possesses a unique set of motivations, making it clear that what fuels one person may not ignite the same passion in another. Instead, cultivating an environment rooted in honesty and transparency lays the foundation for interaction that uncovers the specific drivers of each individual. To foster this type of atmosphere, as a leader, you must extend your openness and candor not only to your team but also to yourself. I recall a conversation I had once, on the topic of workplace motivation, during which someone asked, "Why not simply reward people with more money when they excel?" This question has its merit, and perhaps some of you were anticipating a resounding endorsement of monetary incentives as a prime motivator. Undeniably, money does serve as a motivator, but its effectiveness is bound by time and perspective. Money motivates when it corresponds to immediate needs, just as one feels compelled to seek fresh air in a room deprived of oxygen. Yet, once an individual accumulates sufficient financial resources to fulfill their desires without fear of deprivation, money ceases to produce the same level of motivation. This phenomenon mirrors the nature of financial incentives. Once a person attains a comfortable level of financial security, the impetus to strive for their desired life diminishes. Thus, if money were the sole motivator, we would find ourselves sprinting through the initial five miles of an ultra-marathon only to witness everyone gradually slowing down and dragging their feet by the race's end.

In the year 1985, a pair of American psychologists, Richard Ryan and Edward Deci, dared to challenge the prevailing belief that rewards alone serve as the primary driving force behind human motivation. Their groundbreaking self-determination theory proposed an alternative perspective rooted in intrinsic motivation, which is that the inherent drive for personal and psychological growth resides deep within us all. According to Ryan and Deci, this self-determination comprises three vital components: autonomy, competence, and relatedness.

The Power of Intrinsic Motivation

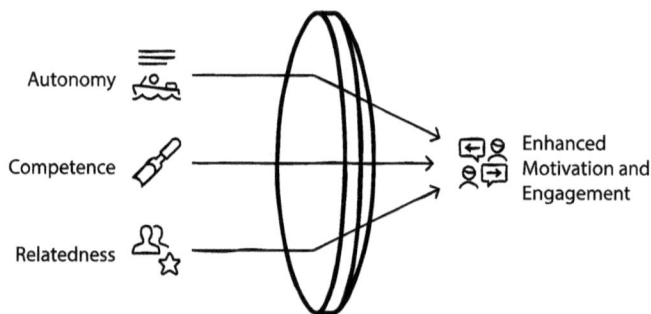

Autonomy, as defined by these visionary thinkers, represents "the desire to be the causal agent of one's own life." When we view the act of granting employees greater autonomy as an avenue for fostering self-determination, remarkable outcomes emerge. Increased levels of satisfaction, fulfillment, and engagement permeate the workplace, for the results achieved are perceived as the fruits of their own innate abilities. Autonomy becomes an intrinsic motivator, propelling individuals to surpass their own expectations and strive for excellence.

Of course, to dismiss the significance of extrinsic motivators such as compensation and benefits would be negligent. Ryan and Deci themselves, as pioneers in their field, certainly appreciated the importance of being duly rewarded for their pioneering work. However, these "controlled" motivators fail to tap into the core psychological elements that truly ignite human engagement and promote exemplary performance. It is precisely why employees, in their quest for motivation, often prioritize the freedom to work flexibly over financial remuneration and other traditional perks.[1]

---

1   Holger Reissner and Dane Fetterer, "Forget Flexibility. Your Employees Want Autonomy," Harvard Business Review, October 29, 2021, https://hbr.org/2021/10/forget-flexibility-your-employees-want-autonomy.

A great example of this implemented within a large establishment is at The Ritz Carlton. At the Ritz, there is a rule which allows each employee to have a stipend of $2,000.[2] This enables them to have autonomy over decisions made in regard to remedying any customer service issue without having to ask the manager. Although this idea may seem simple, it has allowed the Ritz to stay at the top of customer service in their industry. It not only lets the employees feel like they have more independence and free will but also because each employee doesn't have to go through a manager. It also speeds up the customer service experience because the customer is not waiting around for confirmation on whether they can be reimbursed or what have you. They can create a seamless experience for the customer while maintaining their own independence over their decisions.

Fostering Purposeful Action through Motivation

The ultimate goal of motivating people in the workplace is to encourage the right behaviors. You're really motivating them to act in a particular way in order to produce the results that need to be achieved at that company. That's the desired end result for motivation. It's not about getting people excited or dancing in the aisles, it's more along the lines of getting people moving in the right direction. This can all be through individual contribution, team-building, strategic thinking, the list goes on. If we can motivate them towards the right behaviors, then things work out.

Leaders need to find out which incentives work when motivating their teams. Each person is a little different, so not every personality style will align with every motivating factor. Indulge me for a moment. Think of it like you would love languages. Each person will have one or more ways in which they express and like to receive love. Motivators are exactly the same, but instead of love, we're talking motivation.

I want to do a small exercise with you that might help you figure out what things motivate you in the workspace. Think back to the last time you felt a rush of motivation while at work and ask yourself what the cause of this motivation was

---

2   https://crm.org/articles/ritz-carlton-gold-standards.

and how it was sprung on you. Now, keep that in mind as I bring you through the following motivating personality styles.

The Drivers: Drivers are high energy. They're drawn towards outcomes and results, which happen to be their primary motivating factor. They are always focused on the results first and foremost and are highly motivated employees. Although they may not be concerned about how they will get there, their constant mindset is, "I want to get there and I'll do anything to do it." For the Drivers, tomorrow is already too late.

The Harmonizers: The Harmonizers are people who want to achieve results by bringing people together. They make sure to have enough influence over others to get to the end result. They tend to be creative and care more for the 'people' aspect of things rather than the work itself.

The Stabilizers: The Stabilizers are very process oriented. They do their best to carve out a pathway of success for themselves in everything they do—meticulously so. They try to figure out the most efficient way to get to where they want to be, and derive a lot of satisfaction from getting things done. Like a well-oiled machine, they want to create the most efficient way of doing things, day in and day out. A possible downside to this personality is that they are not as thorough because they often tend to be more focused on keeping time than they are on their quality of work.

The Analyzers: Analyzers are your perfectionists. They like to examine a lot of information and data and can sometimes drive people crazy with how particular they can be. You need to give the analyzer space to process and take information in, as this is not someone who is going to be able to give you everything you ask in a short amount of time.

Everyone has dipped into each of these personalities before, but generally, you will gravitate more towards one or two. The idea behind giving you this information is that, as a leader, if you want to motivate anyone, you need to understand them and how they operate in order to really make a difference. Catering to people's needs will not only help a business but build familiarity and trust between you and your team member. If their needs are unmet and their individuality goes unrecognized, it may not immediately tear down the trust between you, but it will not be beneficial in the long run.

The goal here is to recognize and acknowledge people for the behaviors that we want in the way that will mean the most to them. As a result, they will have a tendency to repeat them; that's just human behavior. It is important for the leader to find the right opportunities to recognize behaviors that are going to support success, not only for that person but also for the team as a whole. When thinking about the personality styles, you also want to think about how each of those line up with different ways to show recognition. Your Drivers and Harmonizers tend to be more on the extroverted side, so they will appreciate the more public forms of recognition, while the Stabilizers and Analyzers tend to lean more introverted and will feel more motivated by private and personal acknowledgments. When it comes to demotivators, such as reprimanding someone, it is always, I can't stress enough, always done in private.

Some employees may find money to be a motivating factor for them, and some may not, but whatever the case, monetary motivators need to be delegated with caution in the workspace. The main point I want to drive home with money is that it needs to be handled fairly across the board. People aren't generally worried about being overpaid, and why would they be? More worry and stress stems from being underpaid or paid unfairly. Over the past five years, since the newer generations have taken over more of the workforce, companies have struggled to pay their employees fairly. The new generations share absolutely everything. Once, it used to be frowned upon to share one's income, now it is not uncommon to talk about how much someone makes, which may have an upside. I believe that transparency, just like honesty, is one of the most important things, not just in business, but in life. If talking amongst your peers creates a ripple effect to where we now see companies taking action to provide fair wages, then I think that is only a positive for all and creates a level playing field. Back during the COVID-19 pandemic, the employee marketplace was very soft (difficult to find employees), and companies started to practically throw money at people to come and work for them. Companies are aware of how much more power employees have because of the internet now. If someone feels they are getting underpaid by their employer, they can go home and simply look up what they should be making online.

Imagine telling a company in the 1970s that in only a few decades, their employees will be able to talk to old employees on a virtual page about the positives and negatives of working for your company. I bet they would have made them feel pretty uneasy. Take my son as an example of this extensive caution that many companies are now taking. After receiving his computer science degree, he started working at a fairly high-paying job for an insurance company a few years ago. During the time he has been working there, he has received two unsolicited pay raises that he did not ask for. Curious, he reached out and asked why he was getting these pay bumps and they explained how they had been doing salary surveys to make sure that people were being paid fairly across the board. These precautions enforce more value on labor and instill motivation in a new generation of workers.

The younger generation has been causing some ripples and keeping certain industries on their toes for a while now. The way things are done seems to undergo significant changes with each passing generation, and it can be quite amusing to witness these clashes in the workplace. Younger generations are particularly focused on finding meaning in their work. They want a company's mission and values to resonate with their own beliefs. People increasingly seek fulfillment in their jobs, and when they don't find it, there's a high likelihood of business setbacks due to a lack of motivation. For instance, an environmentalist might not be thrilled to work for companies like Canada Goose or Shell. Surely, there are various reasons why people choose not to work for certain companies. It's crucial to recognize and assess the kinds of individuals who might be attracted to your company and those who might not. Ultimately, people want to take pride in their work and have it contribute to a greater purpose. If the work doesn't align with their core values, it's bound to be a mismatch.

To maintain motivation, you must ensure that your company has goals. Whether it's week to week or month to month, this will inspire people to make their own personal goals. Imagine you take the scoreboard away at a baseball game, who's keeping track? What is the purpose of playing at that point? Keeping score is just like keeping track of goals and setting them when you see fit. When people can't see what is being worked towards, it makes it a lot harder to keep motivation high. It's like going on a drive when you were a kid. You never know how far the drive was so you would always complain, "How much fartherrrrr?" What goal setting does is add a GPS right in front of your seven-year-old self and tell you exactly how long the trip is going to take (as long as there aren't any obstructions that get in the way.)

The number of hours worked doesn't serve as a significant motivator for anyone. What truly drives people is achieving their goals and witnessing tangible results. People crave autonomy in their work. To boost performance, granting autonomy is key, (sometimes) allowing individuals to decide when and where they work. When assigning new responsibilities, clearly defining their scope and level of authority provides a solid foundation. Think of it like running a marathon of 26.2 miles. Imagine reaching the finish line only for someone to ask, "How many steps did you take?" The steps aren't the motivator for marathon runners; crossing the finish line matters. Goals provide focus for individuals and teams, serving as the essential starting point for motivation. Without clear goals, it's challenging to kickstart the engines when people are unsure of the race's endpoint.

A Brazilian entrepreneur, Ricardo Semler, lets his teams decide their own hours. His business is almost completely autonomous; they even get to decide their own salaries and are happier and more productive than ever. It might sound crazy. And how is this possible, you ask? Because they set their own goals and are given the confidence to achieve them. They have ownership. Motivating your team members goes beyond external rewards. It delves into the realm of autonomy and grants them a sense of ownership and emotional investment in their work— an essential ingredient for both individual growth and the prosperity of your business as a whole. When you bestow a new responsibility upon someone, you offer them a profound compliment. It is a testament to their competence and an empowering recognition of their value within the company.

Surprisingly, one of the most underutilized ways to motivate people is by giving them the space and encouragement to learn from their successes and failures. Personal growth is validated through our trials and tribulations. Applying all the principles discussed in this chapter, you shouldn't expect your employees to instantly hit a bullseye from 100 yards. It will likely involve some missteps and learning experiences before they can master the skill. If you can look back at a situation and analyze how you came to succeed or fail, you will be able to grow at twice the speed of someone who keeps tripping on their laces but hasn't looked down to tie them yet. The challenge that many leaders have is that they don't give their team members the opportunity to fail or even make a mistake. This is because these team leaders are holding on too tightly or are thinking about the business as a whole and how, if that mistake were to happen over and over and over again, it could tank the entire company. They don't realize that they are actually doing more damage to the business by tightening their grip than they would if they just stepped back and allowed the employee to learn and grow by allowing them to reflect and self-correct.

At a manufacturing company (known for its innovative products and commitment to quality), I once collaborated with a distinct figure in their organizational structure, Frank, the production manager. Frank epitomized many of the non-motivating aspects we've been discussing. While he was a well-intentioned individual, his management style leaned heavily towards authoritarianism. He often withheld critical information from his employees, inadvertently harming the company's performance and influencing how people executed their tasks. Frank, however, seemed oblivious to the atmosphere he had cultivated, and his unwavering control swiftly thwarted any attempts at self-correction.

The employees under his purview never received performance reports or internal feedback from the company, nor did they glean insights from external sources, such as customers. I once inquired about Frank's approach, asking him why he refrained from providing his employees with feedback and the autonomy to make decisions. His response was telling: "I don't want them to get distracted by all that," he replied. "I just want them to concentrate on the task at hand." It was as if he regarded each team member as a robotic entity, indifferent to their feelings towards the company, himself, their tasks, or anything else, so long as they completed their assigned duties.

A significant challenge within this scenario was the funneling of all decision-making through Frank. He had become a bottleneck, impeding the ability of anyone else to make decisions independently. It wasn't that the employees were unaware of their authority; rather, they had been stripped of any authority they might have had. To alleviate this constrictive environment and liberate the team from the restrictions of centralized control, we adopted a reverse approach. This involved a comprehensive overhaul of the authority structure that Frank had maintained for an extended period. To achieve this, we initiated a process that redistributed decision-making authority across the organization, empowering team members at various levels to make critical choices and contribute to the company's decision-making processes. In other words, like employees at the Ritz with a $2,000 stipend, employees at Frank's organization gained an amount of autonomy that signaled that the organization trusted and encouraged their judgment (but with guardrails). This shift encouraged greater autonomy and fostered a more collaborative and innovative environment, ultimately revitalizing the company's operations and allowing it to adapt more dynamically to changing circumstances.

Key Takeaways & Action Steps

1. **Create a Motivating Environment:** Align values, enhance communication, and empower employees. Set clear directions, make informed decisions, and address mistakes promptly to maintain high morale and productivity.

2. **Understand Individual Motivations:** Recognize that each team member has unique motivations. Cultivate an environment of honesty and transparency, acknowledge hard work, and provide meaningful recognition.

3. **Encourage Autonomy:** Grant employees greater autonomy to increase satisfaction, fulfillment, and engagement. Provide the freedom to make decisions and take ownership of their work, leading to innovation and remarkable outcomes.

4. **Set Clear Goals:** Establish and communicate clear goals regularly. Provide a roadmap for the team to stay focused and motivated, knowing what they are working towards.

CHAPTER 6:

Creating Potential

As a seasoned leadership consultant, I've seen my fair share of workplace dramas, some worthy of a Shakespearean tragedy. But none quite matched the comical chaos I found at a company I will call Masterpiece, which desperately needed an overhaul. Their internal communication resembled a game of broken telephone, and the office vibe was as lively as a library on a Monday morning. While they were well-known for their innovative products, they struggled with internal challenges. Masterpiece's numerous hurdles included a lack of clear communication channels, suppressed employee engagement, and an engrained sense of stagnation.

The company sought to rebuild their workplace culture by investing in leadership development initiatives that would ultimately pave the way for a highly effective and cohesive environment. Recognizing the critical role that effective leadership plays in shaping organizational culture, the company's leadership team also decided to prioritize enhancing their internal leadership structure. Following a reorganization and under the guidance of our tailored leadership development program, the company began to implement a multi-layered approach that emphasized the importance of fostering a culture of open communication, trust, and continuous learning. The program not only focused on honing the skills of the existing leadership team but also emphasized the cultivation of a leadership pipeline, encouraging potential leaders within the organization to step into new roles and responsibilities.

A key driver in this transformation was the implementation of employee coaching and mentorship programs. Employees benefited from personalized one-on-one coaching sessions that defined individual goals and facilitated professional growth. The mentorship program took it a step further, enabling experienced leaders to provide valuable guidance, support, and insights to employees at different stages of their careers. This tailored approach significantly improved employee morale and nurtured a strong sense of belonging and dedication within the organization.

These changes had a real impact. When the leadership team embraced a more inclusive and collaborative approach, employees became more engaged and proactive, significantly boosting productivity and innovation. Improved communication channels also allowed teams to work together seamlessly, fostering a dynamic environment where diverse perspectives were not only encouraged but celebrated. This cultural shift had a noticeable ripple effect on the company's bottom line, resulting in a substantial increase in both customer satisfaction and market share.

The success story of Masterpiece, I believe, is a clear example of the transformative power of investing in leadership development and fostering a culture of coaching and mentorship. Through their commitment to nurturing their internal talent and creating a supportive environment, they not only accelerated their performance but also became an employer of choice. While you might have star performers who shined from day one without additional support, it's crucial for organizational leaders not to leave these outcomes to chance. Leaders should actively foster an environment where all employees have the potential to grow and enhance their skills.

Investing in Your People

You'd be surprised how many companies miss the memo that their greatest potential for success lies within their people. When the CFO is scanning through the company balance sheet, there's no "people" column, right? But here's the kicker: investing in your people, and teams, is what triggers the real magic. When a business is interested in hiring my services, I will initially craft a proposal. This proposal is formulated following a comprehensive understanding of their desired transformations and the type of corporate culture they aim to foster. On occasion, my proposal is met with apprehension masked by a series of questions.

Why, you might ask? Often it is because some business leaders can feel more justified in spending money on the latest sparkling new tech trend or refurbishing the offices and buying a Nespresso machine for the break room rather than investing in their people. Although an investment in talent development has a proven track record of success, you can't touch it and the results are rarely immediate. Unfortunately, our immediate-gratification societal tendencies too often get in the way of doing what is best for the business.

When I suggest to the leadership that they might do better by investing that money in their employees' and teams' professional development or finding other innumerable ways of focusing their investments on their people, the response often ranges from curiosity to confusion. However, overlooking this aspect is a frequent and significant mistake in many business sectors. Building an environment based on trust and motivation, as discussed in previous chapters, lays the foundation for boundless potential and a self-sustaining ecosystem. Emphasizing the critical nature of investing in your workforce, which may involve hiring coaches or enrolling employees in training courses, underscores the profound impact these initiatives can have on overall organizational success. Of course, for many organizations, this falls short. Another overlooked investment lies in leaders dedicating their time and energy to both coaching and mentoring, an integral element often missing in the pursuit of comprehensive growth and sustained performance improvement.

Mentoring and coaching may be similar, but they are also different in many ways. Mentoring someone can be a bit more distant. You could be a mentor to someone and not even necessarily know it. Mentoring is an indirect way of helping someone by encouraging them to emulate you or create similar practices or habits. They reach out, and you give them advice, answers, and wisdom. Then, they go off and try to apply in their own lives some of the things you said.

Coaching, on the other hand, is more deliberate and involved. The student can see the coach almost anytime. A coach is focused on identifying their student's capabilities. They actively consider how to move their student forward and ultimately serve as a catalyst for their student's career.

Let's explore this concept with one of my recent clients, a rapidly growing tech startup with great people potential but lacking in the business and leadership acumen department. As the company expanded, the CEO, Jessica, was committed to nurturing the potential of her team, and she recognized the importance of both mentoring and coaching in achieving this goal.

To address the mentoring aspect, Jessica identified a seasoned industry veteran within the company, Richard, whose success story was well-known in the tech community. Richard became an informal mentor to several employees, offering occasional advice and sharing insights during casual coffee meetings. Employees gravitated towards him, seeking wisdom on navigating the complexities of the tech landscape. Richard's mentoring style was subtle yet impactful, as he inspired his mentees to emulate his strategic thinking and ethical approach to business.

However, as the company continued to scale, Jessica realized the need for a more structured approach to leadership development. Enter Sarah, a Senior Vice President and another industry expert. Sarah is also well known for her proficiency in employee development. With a reputation for driving transformative change, Sarah was engaged to work closely with a select group of high-potential employees.

The coaching sessions Sarah held one-on-one with these high potential employees were deliberate and involved. She conducted comprehensive assessments to identify each individual's strengths, weaknesses, and untapped potential. Unlike mentoring, coaching was a scheduled, ongoing process. Sarah dedicated specific hours to work closely with her clients, setting clear goals, providing real-time feedback, and designing personalized development plans.

The results revealed the distinction between mentoring and coaching. While Richard's mentees gained valuable insights and guidance, Sarah's coached employees experienced a more profound transformation. The coaching sessions were tailored to each individual's needs, focusing on skill development, mindset shifts, and actionable strategies for overcoming challenges. The impact was evident in the enhanced leadership capabilities and increased self-awareness of those who underwent coaching.

In the end, Jessica recognized the complementary nature of mentoring and coaching. Richard's mentorship provided inspiration and role modeling, while Sarah's coaching brought a structured and intentional approach to individual development. Together, these dual approaches created a powerful synergy, propelling the organization toward a future defined by strong, adaptive leadership.

Sometimes, our weaknesses are just a part of who we are, and getting rid of them completely can feel like an uphill battle. An effective coach or mentor doesn't seek to eradicate an employee's weaknesses completely. Instead, they work on those weak spots, strengthening them bit by bit.

But you know what's interesting? Our strengths can become our downfall if we rely too much on them. Take someone who's naturally outgoing and great with people. Sounds like a killer combo, right? Yet if they overdo it, they might come off as a bit too dominating or even egotistical, especially if they're always cutting people off in conversations.

Whether in an official coaching or mentoring capacity or simply by offering informal guidance, your role is to assist team members in discovering their strengths and areas for improvement. The goal is to enable them to leverage their strengths for the company's benefit without allowing these strengths to morph into weaknesses. In essence, your purpose is to support them in addressing challenges head-on, facilitating a faster rate of personal and professional growth than they might achieve independently.

Coaches and mentors have to consider the two main categories that hold people back; capabilities and willingness. These are the two umbrella categories that have the ability to hold every person back. Capabilities may be considered biases, beliefs, skills, or attitudes   that shape an individual's approach to challenges and opportunities. For instance, biases and beliefs can influence decision-making, while skills and attitudes impact how one navigates through tasks and interpersonal relationships. Someone willing to work on improving themselves to gain momentum within a company is bound to see some improvement within themselves and how they perform in the company. However, if the willingness is not there, if they think that where they stand is where they belong and that they aren't good enough for bigger and better things, then there is no chance of improvement. They are stuck on their own shoelace and don't realize why they keep tripping. What tends to happen is that they don't spend time thinking about themselves, about who they want to be, and the things they want to accomplish. This is a huge issue. Without introspection, there is almost no chance of improvement because you are not leaving yourself open to growth.

This is where the power of Emotional Intelligence (popularized by Daniel Goleman in his 1995 book of the same name) becomes vital. It's like possessing a superpower that enables you to delve into your inner self, comprehending how emotions drive your actions and influence those around you. Coaches and mentors should focus on leveraging and fostering emotional intelligence within their teams. This involves guiding everyone to grasp the significance of recognizing their own value and understanding their place in the broader context.

To truly unlock growth and unearth potential, mentors must avoid the ineffective approach of pointing out shortcomings bluntly. Instead, adopting the Socratic method can be immensely effective. Pose questions like, "Do you know what your strengths are?" or "What aspirations do you hold for the future?" Through such inquiries, individuals can navigate their thoughts, uncover blind spots, and arrive at insights independently.

And here's the real magic—listening. A coach (or mentor) opens up a realm of self-discovery for their mentees by simply lending an ear. Through this act of attentive listening, the coach becomes a facilitator, guiding individuals toward a deeper understanding of themselves and their untapped potential. In doing so, the journey of personal and professional growth takes on a more meaningful and self-directed trajectory. This collaborative approach, rooted in emotional intelligence and guided inquiry, ensures that the mentorship or coaching experience transcends mere advice-giving to a transformative force in unlocking the full spectrum of individual capabilities.

Building High Performing Teams

In today's dynamic landscape, the pursuit of highly effective teams is a critical imperative for success. As organizations grapple with the intricacies of collaboration and aim for peak performance, a natural question arises: What distinguishes a genuinely effective team from the rest? How does such a team function, and what sets its leaders apart from those guiding less successful counterparts? The crux lies in the concept of self-governance. When leaders undertake the journey of coaching and propelling their teams to peak potential, they must grapple with three fundamental elements (known as The Team Model) that chart the course toward unparalleled team effectiveness. First is their team's purpose—what is the team responsible for within the company, and what is the job that, from quarter to quarter, month to month, or even week to week, the team is supposed to be doing in order for the company as a whole to succeed? Knowing these basic things about the team's purpose and where the team sits within the company will allow them to have common goals and direction. Self-correcting becomes easier when individuals are aware of their mission and understand what success looks like.

The Team Model – Building High Performing Teams

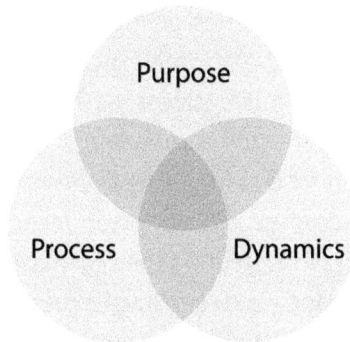

The second thing leaders need to consider is how the team functions or their core process. I frequently encounter this challenge in companies that have transitioned from small startups to larger operations. Due to the lack of standardized operating procedures, new employees often find themselves reinventing the wheel without the necessary operational guidelines. This fragmented approach to tasks hampers overall productivity and severely restricts the company's growth potential.

Lastly, consider the team's dynamics, which directly relate to how team members collaborate. It's all about ensuring trust among them and understanding each person's communication style. The human aspect is incredibly crucial for a team because, without a positive dynamic and robust morale, the team might unravel, and various individuals may get left behind. When the team leader purposefully establishes and coaches these elements, they foster a team environment where everyone comprehends shared direction and goals, the workflow, and how to interact through communication, trust, respect, and constructive conflict. The ultimate goal for every team leader should be to create an environment where team members not only work efficiently but also thrive and grow as individuals.

The Roles Leaders Play

The greatest factor determining a leader's success is their ability to allocate their efforts effectively proportional to how much time they should spend "in" their business versus "on" their business. Leaders are not merely tasked with day-to-day operations and immediate challenges; they must also dedicate significant attention to the overarching strategic vision and long-term goals. The concept of working "in" the business involves hands-on involvement in daily tasks, addressing immediate issues, and ensuring the smooth execution of operational functions. On the other hand, working "on" the business requires a strategic mindset, focusing on innovation, performance improvement, and the development of a clear roadmap for the organization's future. Balancing these dual responsibilities is essential for effective leadership, as it empowers leaders to navigate the complexities of the present while steering the organization towards a thriving and adaptive future. This tricky dance between involvement in the minutiae of daily operations and the strategic elevation of the enterprise defines a leader's ability to foster resilience, innovation, and sustained success in an ever-evolving business landscape.

I'll demonstrate this concept through a construction management company I used to work with, Apex Builders, run by Michelle. She was the brains behind the operation and the go-to person for getting projects done and making sure everything ran smoothly on the ground. You could say she was a pro at working "in" the business, tackling day-to-day challenges, meeting deadlines, and keeping budgets in check.

But Michelle knew there was more to leadership than dealing with the nitty-gritty. She also understood the importance of working "on" the business. So, she started brainstorming with her team between site visits and project reviews. They wanted to take Apex Builders to the next level, not just as a project powerhouse but as a game-changer in the industry.

During one of their strategy sessions, Michelle pitched the idea of making Apex Builders a champion of sustainable construction. While everyone was caught up in the hustle of ongoing projects, Michelle saw a chance to shine in the market by going green. She got her team on board, trained them in eco-friendly practices, and started looking for suppliers who shared their commitment to the environment.

By working "on" the business, Michelle not only secured the success of their current projects but also set Apex Builders on a path toward becoming a leader in environmentally conscious construction. The company started winning contracts based on its sustainability efforts, attracting clients who cared about the planet. Apex Builders went from being a construction company to a socially responsible trendsetter.

Michelle's ability to combine hands-on management with big-picture vision not only boosted the company's reputation but also put it at the forefront of industry innovation. This is a tale of success in which working both "in" and "on" the business creates a winning formula for resilience, innovation, and long-term prosperity.

The Five Roles of Leadership

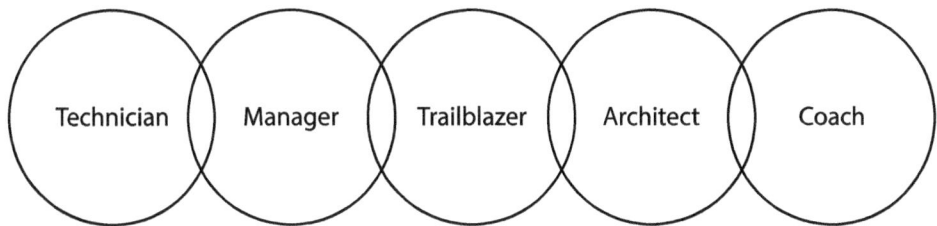

In the world of leadership and management, finding the right balance between handling everyday tasks and planning for the future is crucial for longer term sustainable success. It is a delicate balance of working "in" and working "on" the business. Imagine leadership as a dynamic performance, with leaders shifting between different roles to maintain balance. The Technical and Manager roles focus on working "in" the business, while the Trailblazer, Architect, and Coach roles focus "on" working on the business. Here is a deeper dive into each of these roles:

Technician

Leaders embodying the Technician role showcase an unparalleled technical proficiency, positioning themselves as sought-after experts within their domains. With analytical acumen, they adeptly diagnose and solve problems, relishing the challenge of firefighting. The Technician's hallmark lies in quick decision-making, ensuring operational fluidity and a superior ability to troubleshoot.

Manager

The Manager's role encompasses orchestrating project planning, efficiently allocating resources, and making daily decisions. The Manager navigates the operational landscape by setting goals, tracking progress, completing necessary reports, and maintaining discipline and order. Their mastery extends to seamlessly executing impactful meetings, ensuring organizational alignment and goal attainment.

Architect

As Architects, leaders focus on standardizing processes and aligning them with overarching strategies. They challenge practices misaligned with the organizational philosophy and reinforce positive cultural norms. Architects, keen on continuous learning, engage with others to understand evolving operational methods, shaping a resilient organizational structure.

Trailblazer

Trailblazers possess the acumen to analyze the organizational environment and foresee trends and changes. They articulate a compelling vision for the future and translate it into actionable objectives. Trailblazers foster a culture of innovation by encouraging risk-taking, making connections beyond organizational boundaries, and championing creativity.

Coach

Coaches set high standards for behavior and performance, empowering individuals to make decisions and solve problems. They play a pivotal role in training, development, and conducting performance evaluations. Coaches, acting as team members, actively guide individuals, contribute to their growth, and enhance their effectiveness within the organization.

The Technical and Manager roles focus on day-to-day tasks ("in" the business), being hands-on with immediate challenges. Like a problem-solving expert, the Technician quickly makes decisions to keep things running smoothly. Meanwhile, the Manager plans projects, allocates resources, and maintains order in the organization.

On the other hand, the Trailblazer, Architect, and Coach roles look beyond the daily grind ("on" the business) and aim for long-term success. The Trailblazer spots trends, shares a vision for the future and encourages innovation. The Architect standardizes processes and challenges anything not aligned with the organization's values. They stay up-to-date with new methods to keep the organization strong. The Coach sets high standards, empowers people to make decisions, and helps them grow. In successful organizations, leaders balance these roles, using innovation, vision, and growth as tools to navigate the changing landscape. Mastering all five roles guides leaders to create a lasting success story, smoothly handling both present challenges and future possibilities.

In conventional structures, leaders often emphasize the Manager and Technician roles, addressing immediate operational concerns. However, in high-performance organizations, the spotlight shifts to the Architect, Trailblazer, and Coach roles, paving the way for strategic vision, innovation, and sustained growth. By seamlessly integrating these roles, leaders navigate the present and future intricacies, forging a path towards comprehensive and enduring leadership excellence.

Key Takeaways & Action Steps

1. **Invest in Your People:** Prioritize professional development through coaching and mentoring. Dedicate time and resources to help employees grow, which will improve morale, productivity, and innovation.

2. **Build High Performing Teams:** Establish clear purposes, standardized processes, and positive team dynamics. Foster trust, understand communication styles, and ensure everyone knows their roles and goals.

3. **Balance Leadership Roles:** Effectively balance working "in" the business (daily tasks) and "on" the business (strategic planning and continuous improvement). Play the roles of Technician, Manager, Trailblazer, Architect, and Coach to ensure both immediate and long-term success.

4. **Foster Emotional Intelligence:** Develop and leverage emotional intelligence. Use the Socratic method to help employees discover their strengths and areas for improvement. Actively listen to facilitate personal and professional growth.

Part III

Influence

Mastering Execution and Delivering Consistent Results

In Chapter 7, the focus is on "How to Connect People to Value," connecting your people to your company's value stream, understanding why your company exists, how it delivers value, and addressing common barriers to optimizing that flow.

Chapter 8, titled "How to Measure Success," emphasizes the importance of ensuring people understand how their success is measured, highlighting that what gets measured gets accomplished, the need for both leading and lagging indicators, and the critical role of consistent performance tracking.

Finally, Chapter 9, "How to Create Accountability," focuses on building a culture of accountability, recognizing that holding others accountable is challenging, and ensuring chronic underperformance is addressed promptly.

CHAPTER 7:

How to Connect People to Value

About eight years after I started my business, I signed an agreement with a contract manufacturing company that specialized in making customized component parts for equipment manufacturers in the automation, medical instrumentation, and transportation industries. The company's leadership had communicated to me that the employees working in the manufacturing facility were performing below expectations in terms of quality and productivity. Additionally, they expressed concern about the morale among the employees, indicating that it was notably low. As a prerequisite to facilitating a supervisory skills development program for the manufacturing group, I asked the plant manager for a tour of the facility so that I could gain an understanding of their manufacturing process and the environment where people worked.

The shop floor was organized into manufacturing cells led by a supervisor who was responsible for all aspects of the cell performance with specific emphasis on quality, on-time delivery, and production volume. Moving from cell to cell, I gained a true appreciation for their capabilities, innovation, and expertise in customization. Eventually, we arrived at the end of the production line to the area where they stored the components on hand for their customers. My curiosity grew as I looked at the labeled shelves full of these parts with no names, only numbers.

"So, who do you manufacture these parts for?" I pointed to one of the longer printed numbers on a stack of large parts.

"That's for GE Medical," he said.

"What machine does that go into?" I asked,

"It goes into one of GE's imaging machines." I stopped and thought for a second. If the product this company manufactures, day in and day out, helps detect dangerous abnormalities within the human body, couldn't that be a motivating factor for its team members?

"Who is the supervisor responsible for making that specific part?" I asked. He pointed to a woman in the fourth cell down the aisle and said, "Her name is Lisa."

"And does Lisa know which customer buys this product? Does she know that the product her team produces is part of a machine that can help save people's lives?"

"She has no idea."

I was amazed. I explained to the plant manager that showing the team how their daily work directly contributed to something as important as early detection of health problems could be a big source of motivation. Even though the manufactured components might seem like "just" mechanical parts, the difference between "build this part accurately in a vacuum for your paycheck" and "build this part accurately to help save lives" can change everything. If the facility leaders could connect the dots between what the employees did every day and the impact their efforts had on people's health, the employees would gain a deeper understanding of their contributions and greater meaning from their work. In my mind, this was a clear example of how tying the importance of the final product to the work of those making it can boost motivation, teamwork, and a shared sense of purpose.

Whether your team is crafting components for medical imaging machines or tractors, it's crucial for them to understand the purpose behind their work. Knowing what they are producing and why it is essential for them to derive meaning from their tasks and establish a personal connection to their daily responsibilities. About a month later, when I returned to kick off the training, I made my way onto the manufacturing floor to get a sense of the overall mood among the production staff.

What caught my attention was the placards by each work cell, visually illustrating the application of the product produced. The plant manager had taken my advice to heart. Curious about the potential impact, I asked him if he had noticed any changes since they put the signs up.

"Absolutely! You wouldn't believe it," he said. "It's made a huge difference. Our productivity went up, but specifically, our quality went way, way up. On top of that, we have significantly reduced waste."

Once Lisa and the other team members understood the connection between their contribution and the big picture, they could truly value the work they performed and the products they manufactured.

If you want true execution, consistent results, and lasting impact, you must help people see how their efforts matter—how their work contributes to something bigger than themselves. When people understand their value, the transformation you'll witness will be extraordinary.

Know Your Business Purpose

A typical leading question I ask leadership teams when helping them establish their strategic direction is, "Why does your company exist?" Remarkably, nearly 90% respond with a swift, "Well, to make money." While there's a degree of truth in that response, it's crucial to recognize that money isn't the fundamental "why"; instead, it invariably emerges as a consequence of successfully fulfilling your core purpose. Revenue and profit, in essence, act as byproducts—outcomes derived from consistently and effectively delivering value to the customer. To truly understand why a company exists requires digging deeper into its core purpose and the unique value it aspires to provide. This is accomplished by unraveling the intricate layers of your organization's identity. It involves a comprehensive exploration of your company's mission, vision, and the positive impact it aims to make in the lives of its customers. Beyond financial metrics, the true "why" resides in the transformative value your products or services bring to the market. It's about creating meaningful connections with your customers, solving their pain points, and enhancing their lives in ways that resonate with your organizational ethos.

Communication is very important to foster a culture where every individual, from leadership to frontline teams, is aligned with this core purpose. Leaders must transparently articulate the company's broader mission and explain how each team member's role connects with the greater narrative.

This clarity not only cultivates a sense of purpose but also instills a collective pride in contributing to something beyond the bottom line. Money might spark short-term motivation, but its appeal fades quickly; a raise today leads to the expectation of another next month. It's not a scalable motivator. What really keeps people going in the long run is believing in the company's mission. Take nurses, for instance, dealing with the challenges of healthcare alongside not-so-easy-to-work-with doctors and surgeons. They're not in it for the big bucks; it's about genuinely wanting to care for people. It proves that lasting motivation comes from a deeper connection to a purpose, and is way more powerful than the fleeting allure of money.

A few years back, I held a strategic planning session with a high-tech company specializing in healthcare software solutions. As we worked on defining the organization's vision, mission, and values, I asked a simple question: "What is the number one reason why your business exists?" Although they had a well-defined mission statement and clear business operations, the elusive "why" remained elusive.

As I circled back and forth with the leadership team, I paused the discussion to prompt them further. "You don't directly serve healthcare patients. Your software integrates into healthcare systems. So, what's the value you're providing?" Yet the answer still eluded the team.

"Consider where your solution ends up," I pointed out. "You implement your software into healthcare systems, aiding in the efficient management of patient data, treatment plans, and overall healthcare delivery. It's like planting a seed that grows as long as it's nurtured and maintained. The value you provide is not just about data management; it's about empowering healthcare professionals to enhance patient outcomes and well-being. In essence, you're contributing to the happiness and health of countless individuals, and that's your tremendous value."

Through additional dialogue with the team, this realization clicked—their purpose extended beyond coding and algorithms. They were orchestrating a digital ecosystem that positively impacted lives. Their customers (known internally as healthcare partners) chose how to implement the solutions, tailoring them to their unique needs. The organization wasn't just selling software; it was delivering a platform that fueled healthcare excellence, contributing to the happiness and health of communities.

The key takeaway? Connecting every team member to the overarching "why" aligns them with the broader mission. It's about ensuring that everyone in the company, from developers to support staff, understands the profound impact of their work on the healthcare landscape. It's not just about lines of code; it's about contributing to the well-being of individuals. That understanding fuels collective drive and purpose.

Delivering Value as a Business

Understanding how to connect people to value-delivery is crucial for any organization's success. From my standpoint, all businesses and organizations share fundamental similarities in their operations. If you were to tell a company founder that, they might counter with something like, "No Dave, you're mistaken. Our company is unique; we have distinctive value, a differentiating value proposition," and so forth. I agree, but the fundamental mechanics remain the same beneath those unique aspects, whether you believe it or not.

All businesses function along a defined value chain, with each stage contributing to the value provided to customers—from sourcing materials to delivering the final product. Aligning employees' purpose with this value entails recognizing their roles in this chain. For instance, those in technology development innovate and ensure product quality, logistics teams facilitate timely delivery, procurement professionals contribute to cost-effectiveness, and HR management aligns the workforce with the company's values.

As the examples that opened this chapter illustrate, when employees understand how their work directly influences the company's value proposition, it fosters a cohesive sense of purpose. This alignment strengthens organizational culture and motivates a workforce committed to delivering meaningful products, creating a profound sense of pride and fulfillment among employees.

Porter's Generic Value Chain Model

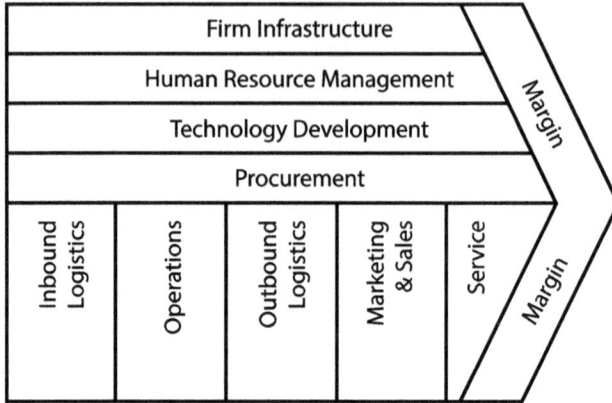

Firm Infrastructure					
Human Resource Management					Margin
Technology Development					
Procurement					
Inbound Logistics	Operations	Outbound Logistics	Marketing & Sales	Service	Margin

This connection between employee alignment and the company's value proposition resonates strongly with Porter's Generic Value Chain Model, further revealing the dynamics at play. As indicated in the model, each functional area represents a distinct link in the organizational chain, working collaboratively to deliver maximum value to customers. For instance, with a technology hardware company like Hewlett Packard, the technological development stage aligns with the model's primary activities related to product design and innovation, ensuring the creation of a unique offering. Similarly, logistics and procurement seamlessly integrate with the model's secondary activities, enhancing operational efficiency and cost-effectiveness. The synergy between the employees' understanding of their roles and Porter's Value Chain Model not only sets the organizational framework but also emphasizes the strategic importance of each stage in delivering a compelling value proposition to customers. It's a holistic approach that reinforces the idea that the interconnection of these activities is integral to achieving sustained competitive advantage and organizational success.

Let's use marketing as a starting point to understand the value chain. Marketing isn't just about flashy ads or big campaigns—it's how you capture attention and spark interest. Whether through digital ads or word of mouth, marketing gets your customers to notice you, kicking off the process that connects every part of your business.

So, you've got people interested. What's next? Sales. Your sales team takes the leads and turns them into actual business. But here's the catch—none of this works if you haven't set the stage with some form of marketing. Sales is the link between the promises made in marketing and the actual delivery of your product or service.

Once the sale is made, it's all about delivery. For services, it could be a consultant showing up and doing their thing. That's the value handed over to the customer. But wait, there's more—customer service kicks in. Customer service isn't just about being nice; it's the key to making sure your customers are happy. If you nail this, there's a good chance they'll come back. And that, my friend, is the sweet spot. It's like welding together all these different pieces—marketing, sales, delivery, and customer service—to create a solid chain of value.

Think of it as a loop. Marketing gets attention, sales make the deal, delivery hands over the goods, and customer service keeps them coming back. Nail this loop, and you've got yourself a strong value chain that people will keep coming back for. It's not just about selling; it's about creating a cycle that customers want to be a part of.

People want their work to have purpose. People don't want to simply punch a time clock and do basic tasks that have no meaning for eight hours every day. They want their work to have merit and for their morals to align with the company's. Individuals in large businesses need to be told and shown how much of a difference their single contribution makes. Once they are given the tools and information to understand this, then that's when you will begin to see change. See, it's a team leader's job to make sure that every person who works at that company is connected to the company's value chain and understands how it works.

I had the privilege of working with a dynamic tech company led by a visionary CEO, Alex. Despite their remarkable success in the industry, a subtle but significant disconnect emerged among the employees. On the surface, everything seemed to be working well, but the daily grind of coding, operations (DevOps), and HR operations (specifically hiring) had become overly mechanical for the team members. As I stated during my initial conversations with Alex, there was far too much "just going through the motions."

During one of our strategy sessions, the realization hit me—there was a need to infuse a deeper sense of purpose into the workforce. This epiphany struck home when I engaged in a conversation with Jessica, a brilliant software developer on the team. She voiced a growing sense of dissatisfaction, feeling like a small cog in a bigger machine. Rather than brushing off Jessica's concerns, I saw it as an opportunity to dissect the workings of the company's operations. Together, Alex and I illustrated the value chain, demonstrating how each team member played an essential role in the larger narrative.

"Jessica," I explained, "your role goes beyond coding. You're crafting the backbone of our innovative solutions. Your work isn't just about programming; it's about creating tools that empower our clients to revolutionize their industries. You're not just a coder; you're an architect of transformation."

As the team began to grasp the broader picture, a shift occurred. The software developers realized their code was the bedrock of the company's unique value proposition. The DevOps team understood that their role was as critical to success as any line of code. HR recognized its responsibility to align the workforce with the company's core values.

This shift in perspective sparked a cultural rejuvenation. The software team no longer saw themselves as mere bug-fixers but as architects of innovation. Logistics wasn't just about moving packages; it was about ensuring clients received a seamless experience. HR wasn't just processing paperwork; they were custodians of the company's culture.

In connecting each employee to the broader value chain, Alex and I reinvigorated the workforce and laid the foundation for sustained success. The collaborative synergy among the teams, reminiscent of the links in Porter's Value Chain Model, streamlined operations and elevated the company's competitive edge.

From my perspective as a consultant, this experience underscores a crucial lesson for business leaders: Understanding and communicating the value chain to every employee can transform a routine job into a meaningful contribution. By intertwining individual roles with the broader business narrative, leaders can inspire a workforce committed to delivering not just products or services but an unparalleled value proposition that resonates with clients and propels organizational success.

Understanding Your Business Process

While the value chain provides the employee with a general connection to the business value, the function area business process takes it to the next level in eliminating ambiguity and making responsibilities and performance expectations crystal clear. To help leaders and teams understand their business process, I always recommend that they conduct a process mapping exercise for all their critical business functions. Business process mapping refers to activities involved in defining what a business entity does, who is responsible, to what standard a business process should be completed, and how the success of a business process can be determined. The main purpose behind business process mapping is to assist the functional areas within a business in becoming more efficient, effective, and scalable. Creating a clear and detailed business process map allows the business to look at whether or not improvements can be made to the current process and how that should happen.

An effective process map acts as a compass, guiding teams, leaders, and employees toward a shared understanding and a unified vision for optimal performance. The functional area business process eliminates ambiguity and crystalizes responsibilities and performance expectations, creating a roadmap for seamless collaboration. When leaders and teams engage in a process mapping exercise for critical business functions, they foster a collective comprehension of what needs to be done, who is responsible, and the standards that should be upheld. This clarity not only enhances efficiency, effectiveness, and scalability but also aligns the entire workforce toward a common goal. The detailed business process map not only serves as a diagnostic tool for current processes but also illuminates avenues for improvement, enabling teams to collectively chart a course towards enhanced business performance.

Process Map Example

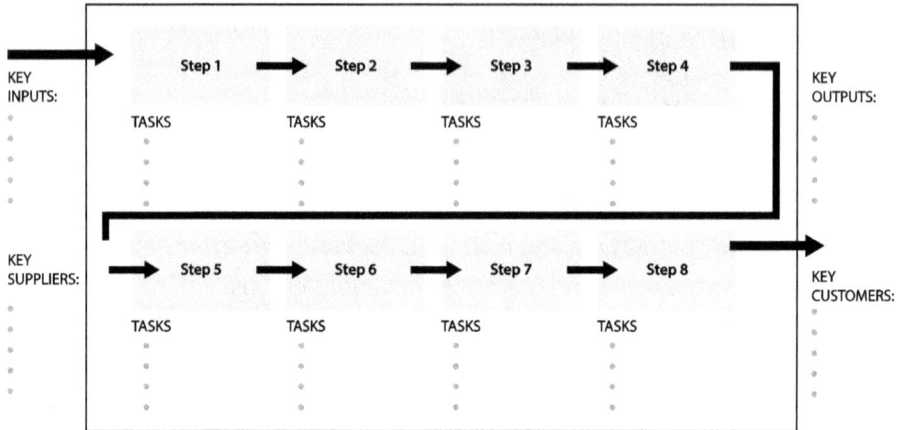

Continuing with the process mapping approach, let's break down the steps to create an effective process map, keeping it straightforward with eight steps or fewer. Complexity can lead to confusion, so simplicity is key. The essential ideas behind a process map are identifying the steps, understanding the major tasks within those steps, and determining the responsible parties.

Before creating the map, it's crucial to define the process. Many groups overlook this step, often rushing through without clarifying each role's responsibilities in reaching the end product. Without proper definition, however, the process risks becoming chaotic rather than a deliberate effort to discuss the most effective steps.

Once you've defined the process, the next step is drawing out the process map. This is an opportunity for team members to clearly understand their responsibilities and authority in the overall process. Questions like "What are my responsibilities?" and "What's my authority in all of this?" can be addressed at this stage. It's essential to ensure that everyone comprehends their roles, the reasons behind their actions, and how improvements can be implemented at each level.

Every process map interprets the core process, breaking it down into interrelated steps and tasks. A comprehensive process map should include key elements such as Unit Operation, Tasks, Inputs, Outputs, Key Suppliers, Customers, Key Customers, and Key Support Groups. This detailed breakdown offers a holistic view of how the process functions from start to finish.

It's important to note that there should be a version of this process map for every department in a company. Without such a map or a comprehensive understanding of it, teams risk losing direction and might struggle to resolve issues when something goes awry in the process.

Now, let's discuss variances—errors, malfunctions, or aberrations in the process that deviate from the normal or expected flow. There are three fundamental types of variances: Inherent, Transported, and Boundary. Inherent variances result from the process itself and are generally within the control of those managing it. Transported variances are passed on from suppliers or others earlier in the process, while boundary variances occur during the hand-off and coordination with other departments, support groups, or customers.

Identifying where the process goes wrong and analyzing these variances allows for quicker problem resolution. Establishing standard responses and solutions creates a robust framework for efficiently addressing recurring issues. This comprehensive understanding of the process and its potential variations is pivotal for maintaining a smooth, efficient, and effective operational flow.

Bottomline: process mapping is like the secret sauce for your business. It's not just about drawing diagrams; it's your GPS for success. Imagine you're the captain of a ship—you need a clear navigational chart, right? Same for leaders and teams! One of my former clients realized their customer service process was causing delays and frustration. By mapping it out, they identified bottlenecks, streamlined operations, and saw a significant increase in customer satisfaction and retention. For example, they discovered that customer inquiries were being routed through multiple departments before reaching the right person, causing unnecessary delays. By reconfiguring the process to direct inquiries to the appropriate department immediately, they reduced response times by 50%. This improved customer satisfaction and boosted employee morale as they could handle issues more efficiently. The company also saw a 20% increase in repeat business, as customers appreciated the swift and effective service. This example highlights how process mapping can transform a business by uncovering hidden inefficiencies and providing a clear path to improvement.

Now, breaking down steps and tasks is like a recipe. You don't cook without knowing what's what. That's how we avoid kitchen disasters and business chaos. And yes, each department has its map. Marketing, sales, and delivery are all different dances but part of the same talent show.

And variances—the hiccups in your plan. Think of them as gremlins (don't feed them after midnight!). Knowing where they lurk helps you eliminate them. Imagine discovering that a small tweak in your process could save hours of work each week. That's the "aha" moment every business craves.

So, what's the takeaway? A simple map and connection to the big picture can be your game-changer. It's not about being formal; it's about making work satisfying, purposeful, and glitch-free. Whether it's creating life-saving widgets or developing innovative software, process mapping brings meaning, unity, and success to any team.

Key Takeaways & Action Steps

- **Connect People to Value:** Help employees understand how their work contributes to the company's success and impacts customers. Use visual aids and clear communication to show the significance of their roles, boosting motivation and productivity.

- **Know Your Business Purpose:** Clearly define and communicate the core purpose of your company beyond making money. Ensure every team member understands how their work aligns with the company's mission and the value it provides to customers.

- **Deliver Value as a Business:** Align employees' roles with the company's value chain. Ensure everyone understands their part in the process, from marketing to customer service, to create a cohesive and efficient workflow.

- **Understand Your Business Process:** Conduct process mapping exercises to define responsibilities, authority, and performance expectations. Identify and address variances to improve efficiency and effectiveness, ensuring all departments are aligned and working towards common goals.

CHAPTER 8:

How to Measure Success

A few years back, I was fortunate to have been hired by Bill, the owner, and president of a well-established manufacturing company, who found himself facing a perplexing challenge. Despite the company's long-standing reputation for quality products, the production floor was experiencing performance inconsistencies, leading to delays in order fulfillment and a decline in customer satisfaction.

Upon joining the company as an executive consultant, I immediately dove into uncovering the root cause of these issues. Through extensive analysis and discussions with the leadership team, it became apparent that the company lacked a comprehensive framework for measuring success and driving improvement. Bill and his team focused on traditional metrics such as production output and financial performance, but did not track key indicators related to customer experience, team culture, process efficiency, and profitability by product.

To address this challenge, I worked closely with Bill and his management team to develop a measurement framework tailored to their operation that encompassed these four equally important areas. We started by identifying key performance indicators (KPIs) for customer satisfaction scores, employee engagement levels, process cycle times, and profitability margins. These KPIs were quantitative and qualitative, ensuring a comprehensive view of the company's performance.

We followed this by implementing a system for tracking and monitoring these KPIs in real time. This allowed us to quickly identify areas for improvement and take proactive measures. For example, when customer satisfaction scores dipped below a certain threshold, we immediately launched initiatives to improve product quality and streamline customer service processes.

Additionally, we focused on fostering a positive team culture by implementing regular feedback sessions and recognition programs. This not only boosted employee morale but also improved overall team performance and collaboration.

As a result of these efforts, the company saw a significant improvement in production consistency, customer satisfaction, and profitability. By measuring success in these four key areas and aligning their efforts accordingly, Bill and his team overcame their challenges and positioned the company for long-term success in the competitive manufacturing industry.

Know the Score

Imagine being a leader in a business where your team isn't aware of how their success is measured. It's like playing a game of soccer without goalposts. Picture a high-stakes match where players are giving their all, dribbling, passing, and shooting. But without goalposts, there's no way to score, no way to know if they're winning or losing. Take that one step further and remove the scoreboard. The game would feel aimless and frustrating. If the players had no way of measuring their success, then what would they be playing for?

This analogy extends to all companies. We need to know how to regularly measure the success of our teams because it motivates individual performance and drives team goal achievement. Simply saying, "I was quite busy this week," doesn't necessarily mean you were successful. You could be busy but working on all the wrong things.

Measuring success, or "knowing the score," is essential in the context of the "team model" described earlier in Chapter 6, which outlines three fundamental elements for building high-performing teams.

First, understanding the team's purpose is crucial. Leaders must clearly define what the team is responsible for within the company and its role in achieving overall success. For example, a marketing team's purpose may be to increase brand awareness and drive customer engagement. Knowing this purpose helps team members align their efforts and work towards common goals.

Also, leaders need to focus on the team's core process or how the team functions. This involves establishing standardized operating procedures to streamline tasks and increase productivity. For instance, a sales team may implement a standardized sales process to ensure consistency and efficiency in closing business deals.

And lastly, team dynamics play a crucial role in team effectiveness. Leaders must foster trust among team members and understand each person's communication style to create a cohesive and high-performing team. Building trust can be achieved through various team-building activities that encourage collaboration and mutual respect. Leaders should also engage in regular, transparent communication, ensuring that all team members feel heard and valued. For example, a team leader might implement regular check-ins and feedback sessions to promote open and honest dialogue. Understanding individual communication styles allows leaders to tailor their approach, enhancing clarity and reducing misunderstandings. By prioritizing trust and effective communication, leaders can create a supportive environment where team members feel confident and empowered to contribute their best work.

By measuring success in these areas, leaders can track progress, identify areas for improvement, and ensure that their teams are working efficiently towards common goals. This approach creates a team environment where members thrive and grow, ultimately leading to higher performance and success for the organization as a whole. Purpose and progress become the foundation for analyzing and making improvements to your team. If your team isn't scoring any goals, how are you supposed to win the game? Keeping score ensures that everyone is aligned with the same objectives and working towards the common goal of the company's success.

What Gets Measured, Gets Accomplished

What gets measured gets accomplished—it's a mantra that rings true in the world of business. So, how can you measure success in your company effectively? Keeping score for your team (this applies to the entire business as well) involves four essential steps: identifying the most critical key result areas, selecting units of measure (known as success measures or key performance indicators <KPIs>) in each key result area, assessing current performances for each KPI, and setting goals to make improvements.

Four Dimensions of Achievement

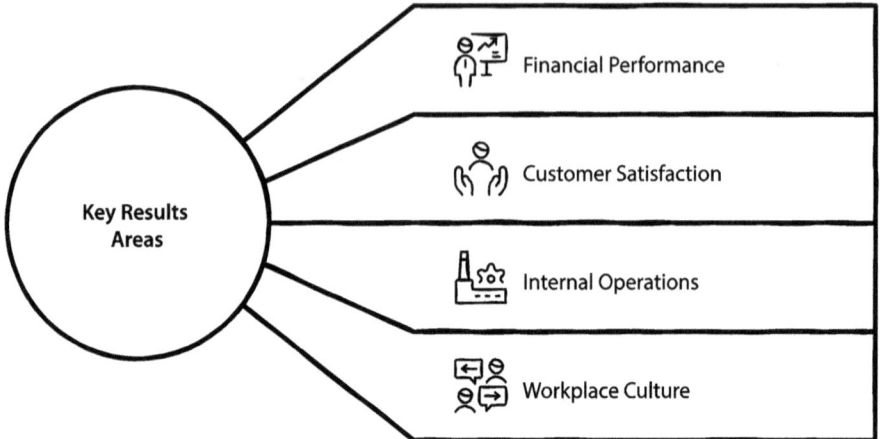

Key results areas can be identified and easily measured across four dimensions of achievement: (1) financial performance, (2) customer satisfaction, (3) internal operations, and (4) workplace culture. Financial performance is a critical area to measure, including aspects like costs, profitability, revenue, and return on investments. Customer satisfaction is equally essential, even for those not directly in customer-facing roles. Everyone in the company, in one way or another, impacts the customer experience, whether it's through their interactions with customers directly or with internal teams (or departments) that serve customers indirectly.

For example, even employees not directly connected to the customer impact customer satisfaction through their work. For instance, a product developer who creates a user-friendly interface contributes to a positive customer experience. Similarly, an efficient supply chain team ensures timely delivery, enhancing customer satisfaction.

Internal operations are another key area to measure, including the company's rate of production, cycle time, employee performance, and the overall efficiencies and effectiveness of processes. Workplace culture (a by-product of leadership and organizational development) is equally crucial, focusing on understanding leadership dynamics, employee motivation, and team development without causing burnout.

In essence, all these areas should be measured in a business to create a balanced measurement system, like a scorecard. By measuring success in these four dimensions, companies can ensure they're on the right track toward achieving their goals and delivering value to customers. This balanced approach to measurement provides a comprehensive view of the company's performance and enables leaders to make informed decisions to drive improvement and success.

Furthermore, a balanced scorecard approach ensures that efforts are not skewed towards one area at the expense of others. For example, focusing solely on financial performance without considering customer satisfaction or internal operations can lead to short-term gains but long-term issues. By measuring success in all four dimensions, businesses can maintain a holistic view of their performance and ensure they're meeting the needs of all stakeholders.

In measuring financial performance, key success measures include profitability margins, return on investment (ROI), revenue growth, and cost-effectiveness. For customer satisfaction, metrics might include Net Promoter Score (NPS), customer retention rates, customer feedback and complaints, and customer lifetime value. Internal operations can be assessed through measures such as production cycle times, defect rates, process efficiency, and inventory turnover. Lastly, for workplace culture, success measures could include employee engagement scores, turnover rates, absenteeism, and alignment with company values.

Overall, measuring success in these key areas is not just about tracking numbers; it's about driving improvement and fostering a culture of continuous learning and growth. When teams understand how their work contributes to these key result areas and see the impact of their efforts, they are motivated to perform at their best and help the entire organization achieve its goals.

Leading and Lagging Success Measures

In Chapter 3, I discussed the concept of leading and lagging indicators as a means to effectively evaluate the performance of your business in order to improve and succeed over the long term. Leading indicators are the ways that we can measure a company's progress, the impact of improvement efforts, and daily achievement, and lagging indicators define success at the moment, looking back to see whether the intended result was achieved.

Here is an example to make my point.

Imagine you're driving a car and want to conserve fuel. The gas gauge in this scenario is a lagging indicator—it tells you how much gas you have left, but only after you've used it. On the other hand, leading indicators would be proactive measures like maintaining a steady speed, avoiding rapid acceleration, and choosing the shortest route—all aimed at reducing fuel consumption. These actions (which can be measured) are like looking ahead on the road to anticipate and mitigate potential fuel-wasting behaviors.

Let's apply this concept to a business. If a company, halfway through the year, is where it needs to be to hit its revenue goals for the year, then that is a success. But, if a company is halfway through the year and is not on track, then it could be too late to make significant changes. Just as, in the example, monitoring fuel consumption helps you adjust your driving behavior to reach your destination efficiently, tracking leading indicators—like sales pipeline metrics, customer engagement, and product development milestones—allows businesses to make timely adjustments to achieve their goals. This proactive approach enables companies to stay on track and make informed decisions to drive success.

Leading and lagging indicators also play a fundamental role in motivating and inspiring employees in a business by providing a clear framework for success and progress. Leading indicators help employees understand what actions and behaviors contribute to success, clarifying expectations and goals. For example, a sales team that knows increasing the number of customer meetings leads to higher sales revenue is more motivated to schedule and conduct meetings. This understanding of how their efforts directly impact outcomes motivates employees to perform at their best.

Lagging indicators serve as markers of progress and achievement, providing employees with a sense of accomplishment. When employees see positive outcomes from their efforts, like meeting or exceeding sales targets, it inspires them to continue working towards success. Lagging indicators can also highlight areas for improvement, motivating employees to strive for better results in the future.

Additionally, leading indicators provide early wins that encourage employees and boost morale. For example, if a marketing team sees an increase in website traffic, it can serve as an early win that motivates them to continue their marketing efforts. Leading indicators also help identify areas where course corrections are needed, enabling employees to make adjustments and stay on track towards achieving their goals.

Likewise, leading and lagging indicators help align individual and team goals with the broader objectives of the organization. When employees understand how their contributions impact the organization's success, they feel a sense of ownership and commitment towards achieving those goals. This alignment fosters teamwork and collaboration, leading to higher levels of motivation and inspiration among employees.

A few years before publishing this book, I was approached by a manufacturing company, let's call them Acme Manufacturing, that had been a local staple for decades but was now facing a downturn in profits, flat revenue projections, and struggling with inconsistent production quality due to rising interest rates and challenges in attracting the right talent. Based on my conversation and interviews with team members, it was clear the company's leadership team was feeling the pressure, frustrated, and not certain on how to turn things around.

As I dug deeper with each team member to gain a better understanding of the functional area operations, it became evident that Acme lacked a systematic approach to measuring and tracking their performance metrics. They were essentially operating blind, unable to pinpoint where they were going wrong or how to improve.

To address this issue, I introduced the concept of leading and lagging indicators to Acme's leadership team. Lagging indicators, such as overall equipment effectiveness (OEE) and customer satisfaction scores, would provide retrospective insights into past performance. On the other hand, leading indicators, such as inventory turnover rate and employee engagement scores, would offer predictive insights into future trends. There was some initial pushback from a couple members of the leadership team, who stated, "We've always done things this way, and it's worked fine for us. Why change now?", and "Implementing these changes will require a significant investment of time and resources. Is it really worth it?"

Fortunately, the CEO was convinced, so building consensus with all team members did not take long. Implementing these indicators was a game-changer for Acme. They discovered that their OEE was significantly lower than industry standards, indicating inefficiencies in their production processes. By focusing on improving these processes, they were able to streamline operations, reduce waste, and enhance overall efficiency.

Likewise, Acme's newfound emphasis on employee engagement yielded remarkable results. As morale improved, so did productivity and product quality. The company also revamped its inventory management practices, leading to optimized inventory levels and reduced costs.

Over time, Acme Manufacturing underwent a remarkable transformation. Profits increased, revenue started to climb, product quality improved, and employee morale reached new heights. This story of Acme's journey serves as a powerful testament to the impact of leading and lagging indicators in driving business performance and fostering a culture of continuous improvement.

Performance Tracking Consistency

Consistently tracking performance is the cornerstone of successful business management. It provides a clear roadmap for progress and improvement. By establishing key performance indicators (KPIs) and regularly monitoring them, leaders can make informed decisions that drive business growth and success.

One of the key benefits of tracking performance consistently is the ability to identify trends and patterns over time. This allows leaders to pinpoint areas of strength and weakness within the organization and take proactive steps to address them. For example, if a certain product line consistently underperforms compared to others, management can investigate the root causes and implement strategies to improve its performance.

Consistent performance tracking also fosters accountability within the organization. When employees know that their performance is being monitored and evaluated regularly, they are more likely to stay focused and motivated to achieve their goals. This can lead to increased productivity, higher quality output, and overall better performance across the board.

From a leadership perspective, consistent performance tracking provides valuable insights into the effectiveness of their strategies and initiatives. It allows leaders to see what is working well and what isn't, enabling them to make data-driven decisions that drive the business forward.

Consistent performance tracking can give employees a greater sense of purpose and direction. When employees understand how their individual performance contributes to the organization's overall success, they are more likely to feel engaged and motivated in their work.

Finally, consistent performance tracking can have a positive impact on customers. By consistently meeting or exceeding performance targets, businesses can build trust and loyalty with their customers, leading to repeat business and positive word-of-mouth referrals.

Consistent performance tracking is essential for driving business success. By establishing clear KPIs and regularly monitoring them, leaders can make informed decisions, foster accountability, and drive employee engagement and customer satisfaction.

It's just like brushing your teeth; research says that you should brush your teeth at least twice a day in order to maintain good oral health, but if you stop brushing every day, you'll run the risk of developing cavities and gum issues. Consistency is key. So, when tracking your performance, if there is a regular cadence that works for the company, team, or individual, you're going to do okay.

Does the executive team need to be looking at the leading and lagging indicators every day? No. But consistency every month or every quarter is imperative for the company to stay on track. Consistency is critical for individuals and teams as well. They should be tracking their performance weekly, if not daily. This is where the team leader comes in; leaders are responsible for making sure that employees understand what it takes for each person to be successful within a team setting. Leaders should try to find the opportunity to give regular constructive, as well as affirmative, feedback so that the individuals know how they are performing.

Many companies just focus on giving lagging performance awards, such as yearly employee appraisals, but this doesn't give the employee much to go off in terms of how to continue getting better and to shift with the company as much as regular, consistent, constructive feedback does.

The CEO of a mid-sized high-tech software company once asked me to coach his VP of Sales, Randy. He was a seasoned and high-energy leader who worked very closely with his sales managers to drive performance within their respective teams. You would not call him a micro-manager, but he was definitely the hands-on type. Revenue performance consistency was another story. Year-over-year growth was too low, and there were major performance differences within the sales manager ranks.

A few weeks into the executive coaching engagement, I centered my focus on Randy's people leadership and coaching skills because of passive aggressive comments he would make about his underperforming managers not taking his instruction. My goal was to shift his perspective from an offensive mindset to one of self-awareness and specifically related to own ability to coach his people. In our next session, I started with a simple question: How does he measure his sales managers' success?

"Well," he said, "It all comes down to the revenue numbers at the end of the year. I just know that if I work very hard and push my people, we will succeed. It's always worked in the past."

"How do they know that what they're doing is effective on a day-to-day or week-to-week basis?" I asked.

After a long pause, Randy stated, "It must be pure instinct based on past experience."

After our conversation, I suggested that he make a request to the CFO to get the data on how each of his sales managers and their respective regions had been performing. The CFO ended up helping Randy and his sales manager understand insights from key data related to each region's booking, billings, profitability, key customer behaviors, and so on—everything they needed to predict future performance results. The simple request of sending Randy to the CFO created a ripple effect; the CFO realized that others at the company were falling short, and she called me a week later to say that it had really been a huge wakeup call to the company.

"We thought that we were pretty good at measuring our business performance. We have all the data, but we clearly have not been doing well enough in sharing with all our managers," she said. The lesson is that everyone should be constantly looking upstream; when you are only looking at what has already happened, there is no way to change those outcomes. However, when you are looking ahead and making predictions, that's when you can shift, dodge, and weave to make sure you hit or exceed your goals.

Provide Access to Data

Access to data and analytics is crucial for all levels of management within a business. Yet, many organizations I've encountered fail to provide full access to their data, or worse, withhold it from employees altogether. This lack of transparency makes it challenging for teams and individuals to track performance and receive timely feedback. After all, how can one know how well they're doing without the means to track and compare their progress?

Even when companies do grant access to data, the next question arises: what are they doing with it? Simply having access to data is not enough; it must be leveraged effectively to drive decision-making and performance improvement. Organizations that embrace a data-driven approach can gain valuable insights into their operations, customer behavior, and market trends, enabling them to make informed decisions that lead to business growth and success.

When it comes to data sharing within organizations, it's important to strike a balance between providing enough information for decision-making and protecting sensitive data. Leaders often need access to various types of data, such as sales figures, customer feedback, and operational metrics, to make informed decisions. However, oversharing sensitive financial details or strategic plans can compromise a company's competitive advantage. For example, sharing detailed financial forecasts with all employees could lead to leaks of confidential information. Similarly, disclosing intricate product development plans to the entire organization could result in premature disclosure to competitors. It's essential to establish clear guidelines on what information should be shared and with whom, ensuring that sensitive data is only accessible to those with a genuine need for it.

By providing access to data and encouraging its use at all organizational levels, companies can foster a culture of transparency, accountability, and continuous improvement. Employees feel empowered when they have access to the data they need to do their jobs effectively, leading to greater engagement and productivity. Additionally, when data is used to drive decision-making, companies can identify opportunities for innovation and efficiency, ultimately leading to better outcomes for the business as a whole.

Key Takeaways & Action Steps

1. **Measure Success Comprehensively:** Develop a measurement framework that includes key performance indicators (KPIs) for customer satisfaction, employee engagement, process efficiency, and financial health. Track and monitor these KPIs in real-time to identify areas for improvement and take proactive measures.

2. **Know the Score:** Ensure that all team members understand how their success is measured. Clearly define the team's purpose, establish standardized operating procedures, and foster trust and effective communication to create a cohesive and high-performing team.

3. **Use Leading and Lagging Indicators:** Implement leading indicators to measure progress and predict future success, and lagging indicators to evaluate current and past performance. Use these indicators to motivate employees, align individual and team goals with organizational objectives, and drive continuous improvement.

4. **Provide Access to Data:** Ensure that all levels of management have access to relevant data and analytics. Use this data to drive decision-making, foster a culture of transparency and accountability, and empower employees to track their performance and make informed decisions.

CHAPTER 9:

How to Create Accountability

One of my long-term clients experienced a very difficult issue, that plagued many businesses during the COVID-19 pandemic, and that was trying to ensure that they minimized productivity losses with their entire staff working from home. This was a project-based business that relied heavily on collaborative and cohesive teamwork to ensure they deliver the highest value to every client. Without face-to-face interaction, the CEO and her leadership team feared that innovation and creativity would suffer and accountability to results would drop off dramatically. I recommended to the CEO that she allow things to play out for a few months and then look at some of their key success indicators related to productivity before they made any bold moves, which she agreed to.

An important part of this story is the CEO's default management and leadership style, which leaned toward command-and-control. In the previous year, I had been very successful in coaching her to moderate that tendency and rely more on an empowering approach, a shift welcomed by her leadership team and employees. The change in her behavior was not immediate, but the longer-term impact on the business was clearly noticed in the form of increased morale, the willingness of people to make decisions, and an increase in results ownership.

Roughly three months into the pandemic, I could tell the CEO was getting anxious and stress cracks were starting to show. As her coach and advisor, we stayed in touch regularly, but the pressure became too much for her after a quarterly review of their key performance indicators, which revealed a slight degradation in productivity related to utilization targets. In this situation, utilization refers to the measure of how effectively resources (personnel hours) are being used to complete project tasks. It was typically expressed as a percentage and calculated by dividing the actual amount of time a resource is productively working on project tasks by the total available time for that resource. High utilization rates indicate that resources are being used efficiently, while low utilization rates may suggest underutilization or inefficiencies. In the CEO's mind, this immediately translated into a lack of accountability and lower profits.

This stress pushed her back to her default style and resulted in a reactive decision designed to increase accountability by very closely monitoring (a.k.a. micromanaging) people's hours for fear that the employees were cheating the company out of valuable time. As you can see from where this story is going, it did not have the desired effect. In fact, it made the situation worse. The top performers in the business perceived the micromanagement as an insult to their dedication and strong work ethic, and many others responded by contributing just the forty-hour minimum when historically they would put in much more. They got a marginal increase in hours from the average employee group but nothing of real value, and the overall results lowered the quality of work, morale, and value to their clients. They had to reverse course.

I worked with the CEO and her team to build consensus on the best approach for their business model and to increase project team accountability without micromanagement. We focused on setting clear expectations and goals, empowering team members with autonomy, and using collaborative tools for transparent tracking. Regular check-ins were scheduled to provide support rather than control, and we encouraged open communication. Recognizing achievements and ensuring team members had the necessary skills and resources to succeed were also key components of our strategy. It was a temporary setback, but in short order, morale improved, and accountability was restored.

Build A Culture of Accountability

The term accountability can often stir up anxious emotions in people. Nobody wants to hold anyone accountable because it involves difficult conversations and uncomfortable situations just as much as no one wants to be held accountable because it's embarrassing to be called out. In my opinion, this can be said for well over 50% of the population. I see it all the time. The other half of the population has figured out a way to hold people accountable that works for them, but most of those people still don't enjoy doing it. For most of the leadership assessments I have conducted over the years, "lack of accountability" makes the top five list of prevailing weaknesses and factors affecting poor business performance. And in a high percentage of these situations, it is not just a handful of leaders at fault; it tends to be more broad-based and part of the organization's cultural norms.

A company's culture is the experience employees have while working there, shaped by its core beliefs and everyday attitudes. Though culture is not easy to change, leaders directly influence it. In a culture of accountability, employees take ownership of results and their corresponding actions, and hold themselves accountable. When mistakes happen, defensive reactions are rare. Instead, employees embrace ownership and responsibility, willing to learn from their errors, and work diligently to resolve issues.

But how do you create a culture of accountability? What does that look like? It might not be exactly what you initially picture—constantly monitoring and calling out every employee for each little mistake. Instead, leaders set the tone and standards for accountability by establishing clear expectations and fostering an environment where people feel comfortable speaking up, asking questions, taking ownership, and not fearing failure. This approach encourages employees to hold themselves accountable, reducing the need for constant oversight.

In a strong culture of accountability, people are engaged, take responsibility, and use their discretion wisely. When something isn't going right, they say, "I don't like this and I want to fix it," or, "Here's the solution." There's no, "Well, that's not my job." Instead, people understand the balance between respecting others' responsibilities and stepping up when needed. For example, if Department A serves Department B and something isn't working, the leader needs to clearly articulate what needs to be fixed and how both departments can avoid similar issues in the future.

This environment of mutual respect and proactive problem-solving creates a dynamic where everyone is committed to the organization's success. People are motivated to contribute their best, knowing that their efforts are recognized and valued. In turn, this leads to a more efficient, productive, and positive workplace where accountability is a shared value and responsibility.

Furthermore, creating a culture of accountability requires consistently reinforcing these principles. Leaders must model the behavior they expect to see, provide regular feedback, and recognize those who take ownership of their actions. It's not just about addressing problems when they arise but also about celebrating successes and learning from failures.

Transparency and open communication are key components. When leaders openly share information and the rationale behind decisions, they build trust and help employees understand the bigger picture. This transparency enables individuals to see how their roles contribute to the organization's goals and empowers them to take initiative.

Accountability also involves setting measurable goals and regularly reviewing progress. When employees know what is expected of them and how their performance will be measured, they are more likely to stay focused and motivated. Regular check-ins and performance reviews provide opportunities for constructive dialogue and course correction.

Ultimately, a culture of accountability is one where everyone is committed to the collective success of the organization. It fosters a sense of ownership and pride in one's work, encouraging continuous improvement and innovation. When employees feel responsible for their outcomes and are supported in their efforts, the entire organization benefits from increased efficiency, productivity, and morale.

Leaders create a culture of accountability by:

1. **Setting Clear Expectations:** Clearly define roles, responsibilities, and performance standards. Ensure everyone knows what is expected of them and how their work contributes to the organization's goals.

2. **Leading by Example:** Demonstrate accountability in their actions and decisions. Leaders should model the behavior they expect from their team members.

3. **Providing Regular Feedback:** Offer constructive feedback and recognition regularly. Address issues promptly and praise accomplishments to reinforce positive behavior.

4. **Encouraging Open Communication:** Foster an environment where team members feel comfortable discussing challenges, asking for help, and providing updates without fear of retribution.

5. **Empowering Employees:** Give team members the autonomy to make decisions and take ownership of their work. Trust them to manage their tasks while providing support and resources as needed.

6. **Implementing Transparent Processes:** Use clear and consistent processes to track progress and hold individuals accountable. Ensure that everyone has visibility into how their work impacts the team's success.

7. **Offering Support and Resources:** Provide the necessary tools, training, and resources for team members to perform their duties effectively. Invest in their development to build competence and confidence.

8. **Aligning Goals and Incentives:** Align individual and team goals with the organization's objectives. Use incentives and rewards to motivate and reinforce accountability.

Foster Engagement

In the Venn diagram of leadership and accountability, there is a sweet spot where things flow without getting stuck. A place of ease called employee engagement fueled by empowerment from effective leadership.

Employee Engagement

When I coach people on empowerment, the first thing I remind them is that the word right in the center of empowerment is power. Leaders need to delegate or share their power. Not all of it, but just enough of it so people feel empowered by their own responsibilities. Empowerment is a feeling for many people, and it enables and encourages individuals to recognize and utilize their own inherent power, skills, and abilities. It involves creating an environment that fosters autonomy, trust, and confidence. Engagement and empowerment cannot be imposed on people, it is a result of the conditions that they are in and the environment that a leader creates. The center of any business is its engagement because the behaviors that come from being engaged or empowered are, on a personal level, ownership and accountability and, on a team level, self-governing.

Timely and Consistent Accountability

Creating a culture of accountability is not an exact science. There are times when you must have those difficult conversations when an employee is consistently underperforming. As a leader, it is your responsibility to ensure that team members meet the expected level of performance. In any business, you won't have only all-star players. You'll have a few A performers, a majority of B performers, and a few C performers lagging behind. On a bell curve, your B performers will form the hub, with A performers being the high achievers, and C performers needing either to be motivated to improve or to be let go to avoid dragging down the team.

When individuals are underperforming, even in their basic responsibilities, having those tough accountability conversations is crucial. While difficult and often personal, these discussions are essential. When I ask leaders, "Why didn't you address this earlier?" the typical response is, "I hoped they would realize their mistakes and improve on their own." This sets a dangerous precedent; if underperformance goes unaddressed for months, it becomes normalized.

Allowing issues to fester makes the eventual conversation harder for both parties, as it implicates both the leader and the employee. This is where leadership courage is vital. You need to tell yourself, "I have to address this, and I have to do it promptly." Address underperformance as soon as you see it. Letting it linger for months affects not only you and the employee but potentially the entire organization. Overcoming the fear of having these conversations with your team will yield significant benefits.

If a company tracks and measures its successes accurately, employees will be able to recognize when they are underperforming because they can compare their performance against clear benchmarks. Expectations for outcomes and results must be explicitly stated and understood, making data tracking and measurement meaningful only when employees have access to this data themselves. Performance tracking without transparency renders the data useless.

I've often seen situations where an employee struggles with a task, and a manager merely says, "Hey, I think you're struggling here. You really need to sort it out." This approach is ineffective because it doesn't provide enough guidance. The employee remains stuck with the same issue, now compounded by the pressure of vague and unhelpful managerial feedback. Instead, employees need clear, actionable insights and access to performance data to truly understand and improve their performance. For example, "Hey, I think you're struggling here with meeting deadlines, and I think it may be an issue with how you prioritize your work. Let's work together to figure out a better approach."

Diagnose Performance Issues (Before it is too late)

Over the years, I've seen many clients struggle with recognizing and addressing performance issues before they spiral out of control. One particularly memorable case was with a small machine tool company that prided itself on its customer intimacy but was having a tough time with the performance of its customer service manager, Todd. He replaced the previous manager who left the company, and Todd had been in the position for a little over a year when I was asked to coach him due to his inconsistency and follow-through on commitments.

The company president told me that his colleagues were extremely frustrated, customer complaints were on the rise, and this had been going on for more than six months. Why they let this go on for so long was a mystery at the time but became very clear after I completed my initial assessment of the situation. What was initially believed to be a simple lack of prioritization and organization, was in fact much more serious. Todd was way over his head in experience and skills, and he lacked the desire (a willingness issue) to accept any help. These issues were compounded by the company's misunderstanding of the root cause issues and lack of action in confronting the situation earlier when there may have been a better chance to convince Todd to accept some help. It was too late.

Recognizing underperformance is straightforward; however, understanding its root cause is more complex. When diagnosing underperformance, it's essential to delve deeper into the underlying factors that may be contributing to an employee's struggles. In my experience, there are four key areas that often play a significant role: expectations, skills, resources, and attitude. By thoroughly examining each of these areas, we can gain a comprehensive understanding of the issues at hand and develop effective strategies to address them.

1. Expectations

Expectations form the foundation of performance. Without clear, communicated expectations, employees are left to guess what success looks like, leading to confusion and inconsistent results. Effective expectations should be specific, measurable, attainable, relevant, and time-bound (SMART). This clarity helps employees understand exactly what is required of them and how their efforts contribute to the broader goals of the organization. Regularly revisiting and reinforcing these expectations ensures alignment and allows for adjustments based on changing circumstances.

2. Skills

The next point I consider is whether the individual has the appropriate skills to perform their role. Skill requirements vary depending on the specific job, ranging from technical skills to social awareness. Identifying any skill gaps is crucial for addressing underperformance. For instance, an employee might lack the critical technical skills required for their tasks, which can be addressed through targeted training or mentoring. On the other hand, they might need to improve their interpersonal skills to better collaborate with colleagues. Conducting a thorough skills assessment helps pinpoint areas for development, enabling you to provide the necessary support and resources to help the employee succeed.

3. Resources

The third point I examine is resources. Does the individual have access to the necessary resources? This includes information, reports, technology, company data, and access to knowledgeable colleagues who can assist with questions.

Lack of resources can significantly hinder performance. For example, an employee might struggle to complete tasks efficiently if they lack the proper tools or information. Ensuring that employees have what they need to perform their jobs effectively involves regularly checking in on resource availability and addressing any gaps. Providing adequate support systems, such as mentorship programs or collaborative platforms, can also enhance resource accessibility and utilization.

4. Attitude

Finally, I assess the individual's attitude. This is crucial because an unhelpful attitude can severely impact performance. If someone is unwilling to perform certain tasks, learn from superiors, or grow, they become a lost cause, mentally checked out of their role. A positive attitude, on the other hand, fosters resilience, adaptability, and a willingness to take on challenges. To address attitude issues, it's important to understand the underlying causes, ranging from personal dissatisfaction to misalignment with the company's values. Open, empathetic conversations can help uncover these issues and facilitate a more positive outlook. Encouraging a culture of continuous learning and recognition can also promote a more constructive attitude towards work.

By addressing these four areas—expectations, skills, resources, and attitude—you can more effectively diagnose and resolve underperformance issues, ultimately fostering a more productive and engaged workforce. Ensuring that each aspect is thoroughly evaluated and addressed will help create a supportive environment where employees can thrive and contribute to the organization's success.

Sustain and Enhance Accountability

Creating a culture of accountability is one thing, but maintaining and enhancing it over time? That's a whole different ball game. This is where continuous improvement comes into play. Think of it as regularly tuning up your car to keep it running smoothly. We can't just set it and forget it; accountability requires regular feedback and review cycles. Just like how your favorite TV or Netflix series keeps you hooked with new episodes, we need to keep our employees engaged with ongoing feedback and performance reviews. This way, we can adjust goals and expectations as needed, ensuring everyone stays on track.

But wanting accountability alone isn't enough, you'll need best practices to achieve your desires. Employees want and need training and development. Investing in your team's growth is like adding new skills to your gaming character—it makes everyone more effective and adaptable. Whether through workshops, online courses, or good old-fashioned mentoring, providing opportunities for skill enhancement is crucial. Encourage your team to embrace lifelong learning because, let's face it, nobody ever complained about having too many skills in their arsenal.

And who doesn't love a good pat on the back? Recognition and reward systems are vital. Celebrate successes and milestones, big or small. Implement a fair and motivating reward system that ties directly to accountability and performance. After all, even the smallest victory deserves a high five, a gold star sticker (or even a small bonus).

Change is the only constant in the business world, and adaptation is key. Stay agile and encourage innovation within your team. Regularly evaluate and refine processes to keep things fresh and efficient. Think of it as spring cleaning—getting rid of what doesn't work and making space for new, better habits.

Lastly, let's not forget about leadership development. Developing leaders who model accountability is like having a team of superheroes leading the charge. Provide leadership training and mentorship to ensure your leaders are well-equipped to support their teams effectively. After all, a great leader can inspire an entire team to achieve the seemingly impossible—like turning a struggling company into a market leader.

By focusing on continuous improvement, you ensure that accountability isn't just a one-time project but an ongoing journey. Keep the momentum going, and you'll build a resilient, high-performing team ready to tackle any challenge.

Key Takeaways & Action Steps

1. **Build a Culture of Accountability:** Set clear expectations, foster an environment where employees feel comfortable speaking up, and encourage ownership and responsibility. Leaders should model accountability, provide regular feedback, and recognize achievements to reinforce positive behavior.

2. **Foster Engagement and Empowerment:** Delegate power and responsibilities to employees, creating an environment that fosters autonomy, trust, and confidence. Address underperformance promptly and provide clear, actionable insights to help employees improve.

3. **Diagnose Performance Issues Early:** Regularly assess expectations, skills, resources, and attitudes to identify and address performance issues before they escalate. Provide necessary support and resources to help employees succeed.

4. **Sustain and Enhance Accountability:** Implement continuous improvement practices, provide ongoing training and development, and establish recognition and reward systems. Encourage innovation and adaptability, and develop leaders who model accountability.

Conclusion

As we reach the final pages of this book, we've navigated through various key areas on what it takes to become a more effective leader. But before you close the book and move on, I encourage you to pause and take a step back. With the fresh perspective you've gained, it's time to ask yourself some tough questions: What are the underlying causes of dissatisfaction in your organization? Where do these issues originate, and how can they be resolved? Challenge yourself to create scenarios where you apply the advice and tools we've discussed. By conducting an honest self-assessment, you'll gain a clearer picture of where you stand today, and only then can you begin to drive real, meaningful change.

If you want your team (and organization) to reach its full potential, both you and your team members must be willing to set aside your egos and embrace vulnerability. This means being open to feedback, admitting when you don't have all the answers, and creating an environment where your team feels safe to do the same. Vulnerability is often seen as a weakness, but in reality, it's a powerful tool for building trust and fostering genuine collaboration. When leaders show that they're human, make mistakes, and are open to learning, it sets the tone for the entire organization. Your team will be more likely to take risks, share ideas, and contribute their best work because they know they won't be judged harshly for stumbling along the way. This openness paves the way for innovation, stronger relationships, and a culture where everyone is committed to continuous improvement. In the end, it's not about being perfect; it's about being authentic and creating a space where everyone feels valued and empowered to grow.

Take a moment to reflect on the leadership dynamics within your organization. Consider what's working well and where there might be room for improvement. Are there forces propelling your leadership forward, or are there obstacles holding it back? Understanding these dynamics is crucial to driving meaningful change. By systematically assessing these factors, you can create a clear, actionable path to elevate your leadership effectiveness.

One powerful tool to help you with this is the Force Field Analysis, which allows you to identify and address the forces at play in your organization. As you move forward, don't forget to apply the steps outlined at the end of each chapter to reinforce and build on the strategies discussed.

The Force Field Analysis is a powerful tool for assessing and improving leadership effectiveness within an organization. Originally developed by Kurt Lewin, it identifies and analyzes the forces that drive or hinder progress toward a goal. When applied to leadership effectiveness, it helps you understand the factors supporting strong leadership and those holding it back.

Here's how you can use a Force Field Analysis to assess an organization's leadership effectiveness:

1. Define the Goal

Start by clearly defining "leadership effectiveness" for your organization. This could be a specific goal, such as improving team collaboration, enhancing decision-making processes, or increasing employee engagement. Be as specific as possible so that the analysis has a clear focus.

2. Identify Driving Forces

Next, list all the forces that are currently driving effective leadership within your organization. These are the factors that support your goal. They might include:

- **Strong Communication:** Leaders who effectively communicate the vision and expectations.
- **Empowerment:** Leaders who delegate authority and encourage autonomy.
- **Trust:** A culture where leaders and employees trust each other.
- **Ongoing Development:** Access to leadership training and development programs.

3. Identify Restraining Forces

Now, list the forces that are restraining or hindering leadership effectiveness. These are the obstacles you need to address. Some common restraining forces might include:

- **Lack of Clarity:** Unclear roles and responsibilities among leaders.
- **Resistance to Change:** Leaders or employees who are resistant to new ideas or processes.
- **Micromanagement:** Leaders who are overly controlling and do not empower their teams.
- **Low Morale:** A negative work environment that demotivates leaders and teams alike.

4. Analyze the Forces

With both driving and restraining forces listed, the next step is to analyze them. Consider the strength of each force and how much it impacts leadership effectiveness. To visualize the most significant factors, you might rate each force on a scale (e.g., 1 to 10).

5. Develop Strategies to Strengthen or Reduce Forces

- **Strengthen Driving Forces:** Look for ways to amplify the forces that are already contributing to effective leadership. For example, if strong communication is a driving force, consider investing in more communication training or tools.
- **Reduce Restraining Forces:** Identify strategies to minimize or eliminate obstacles. If resistance to change is a significant barrier, you might focus on change management training or involve leaders in the change process to increase buy-in.

6. Create an Action Plan

Based on your analysis, develop an action plan that outlines specific steps to strengthen driving forces and reduce restraining forces. Assign responsibilities and set timelines for each action to ensure that progress is made.

7. Monitor and Adjust

Monitor progress regularly as you implement your action plan. Leadership effectiveness isn't static, so it's important to periodically reassess the forces and adjust your strategies as needed. The Force Field Analysis can be revisited to ensure that new challenges are addressed and that the organization continues to move toward more effective leadership.

By systematically using the Force Field Analysis, you can gain a clear understanding of the factors influencing leadership effectiveness in your organization and create targeted strategies to enhance leadership and drive organizational success.

Now that you've got a solid grasp of how to use force field analysis to assess and boost leadership effectiveness, let's take a moment to zoom out and consider the bigger picture. We've covered a lot of ground in this book—everything from building a culture of accountability to fostering employee engagement and tackling performance issues head-on. Each of these components is a piece of the puzzle that shapes strong, effective leadership.

As we move into the next few paragraphs, I'll walk you through some of the key points we've discussed throughout this book. These are the essential takeaways that can help you drive meaningful change in your organization and elevate your leadership game. So, let's revisit these crucial concepts and see how they all fit together to create a powerful, cohesive approach to leadership.

The first thing we tackled was the simple truth that most leaders overlook: the working environment (your culture) is actually pretty straightforward. Yet, many company leaders don't take the time to really study and understand the fundamentals of their teams and cultural dynamics. This lack of attention makes it hard to spot the early signs of stress within the organization. That's why we kicked things off with a deep dive into the importance of performing a self-assessment as you start your journey toward becoming a better leader.

Then, in Chapter Two, we moved on to one of my favorite topics: "Managing vs. Leading." Understanding the difference between these two roles is crucial. They require distinct skills, each requiring time and experience to master. Without both, you become a lopsided leader, and your company will feel the effects. Leadership is all about creativity, connection, and courage, while managing is more analytical, demanding experience with people and proper training.

Next up, we explored how to create direction within your organization. Remember the analogy we used? People need a roadmap. Without it, they get lost. You wouldn't send someone on a cross-country trip without a map, right? The same goes for your team. When you provide clear direction, you naturally boost employee engagement. They require less energy from you because they're not constantly scrambling to solve problems—they already know the path to take. As a leader, your ability to communicate this direction is key. If you can't clearly convey the course, you've already lost your team. It's all about delivering accurate information in a way that's easy for everyone to understand, so the entire organization is aligned and moving toward the same goals.

We also covered the essential topic of establishing trust within your organization. Being trusted and respected as a leader is non-negotiable—without it, you have no influence. Trust is like the oil in an engine; without it, everything grinds to a halt. Sometimes, we tear down trust without even realizing it, often due to miscommunication. The bottom line? Trust is built between people. It's that intangible vibe you get from a group, often shaped by the actions of just a few individuals. While trust doesn't develop overnight, you can start by being trustworthy yourself.

After creating trust, we can then create motivation. The essence of motivating your people boils down to only a few points. You can't force people to be motivated because they are either intrinsically motivated or not. They're not objects you can trick into productivity; it's about creating the conditions that allow people to be motivated. Leaders must attempt to create good, strong, one-to-one relationships between each of their employees. Factors that drive motivation falls into areas of:

- Success
- Goal achievement
- A sense of belonging
- A sense of purpose
- Feeling valued
- Being recognized
- Collaboration
- Opportunity for professional development and growth
- Being paid for performance

Remember that each employee is motivated differently, and what works for one may not work for another. This is why it is so important to learn about each employee as an individual and nurture a one-to-one relationship with them. By doing this, you will better understand them.

We explored how to help your employees nurture the seeds of potential they each carry. Far too often, businesses overlook the potential within their people. Growth doesn't come just from a pat on the back—it requires self-reflection and discovery. There are two main barriers to unlocking potential: willingness and capabilities. Capabilities can be taught, but willingness? That's something an employee has to bring to the table themselves.

Next, we discussed the importance of connecting people to the value of the company. Making sure your employees feel truly connected starts with helping them see how their contributions matter. When employees have some skin in the game, they develop a personal attachment to the company. If you want to get the best out of your team, they need to understand the significance of their efforts. Unfortunately, many companies don't spend the time to make this connection clear, and it shows—in the form of higher turnover rates and disengaged employees.

We also talked about measuring success. This is crucial because, without something to measure against, how can anyone know where they stand? It's like playing a sport without a scoreboard—there's no excitement, no sense of achievement. If your employees don't have a way to track their progress, how can they stay motivated? You can't expect someone to keep pushing at 100% if they don't know how far they've come. That's a fast track to burnout.

Finally, we tackled the tough topic of establishing accountability within your organization. Accountability can be tricky because, let's face it, no one enjoys confrontation. But when it's done right—honestly, openly, and early in the relationship—it can be one of the best tools for strengthening your organization.

As a leader, you're the mirror your team looks into. Your strengths and weaknesses are reflected in the company's operations. Confident and competent leaders who invest time and energy into their people will see the returns in the form of a dedicated and driven team. No matter how much advice I've given you, nobody knows your company better than you do. You're the one who understands how it ticks, where it shines, and where it stumbles.

The goal of this book is to help you keep your company at its best. Take in all this information, revisit it as often as you need, and use it to fine-tune your leadership skills. This book is your tool to unlock the full potential of both you and your company.

Acknowledgements

I owe a deep gratitude to all my clients over the past 23 years. Your confidence and loyalty have not only driven my business but inspired me to continue growing and evolving. Without you, this book would not exist.

To Laurie McDowell – your persistence and gentle nudging pushed me to finally sit down and get this book written. Thank you for believing in this project even when I was unsure of it myself.

Jill Brown – a huge thank you for keeping the business back office running smoothly, freeing up the time I needed to focus on writing. Your support behind the scenes was invaluable.

To Ken Lizotte CMC and Elena Petricone at the Emerson Consulting Group, inc. – your patience and encouragement made the editorial process so much easier, and your coordination was instrumental in getting this book across the finish line.

Cindy Murphy – for the fantastic graphic and design support. Your creativity brought the book's visual aspects to life in ways I couldn't have imagined.

Finally, to my mastermind group – Andrea Fredrickson, Kevin Berchelmann, Randy Boek, and Richard Fagerlin – you've inspired me in more ways than I can count. From pushing me to be my best, to giving me the confidence to take on this big project, and and of course, for all the laughter-filled dinners. I couldn't ask for a better group to lean on.

Simplicity Driven Leadership

About the Author

David Liddell is a seasoned leadership consultant with a remarkable career spanning over three decades. As the founder of Liddell Consulting Group LLC, he leads a team dedicated to delivering customized solutions that enhance operational efficiency and drive continuous improvement. David's client-centric approach, combined with his deep understanding of diverse industries, has transformed countless businesses, reshaping their strategies for long-term, transformative growth.

A recognized thought leader, David has been featured in numerous prominent publications and is a frequent speaker at conferences, where he shares his insights on strategic leadership, change management, and organizational transformation. His passion for leadership development extends beyond his professional work—David actively engages in philanthropy and is committed to mentoring the next generation of leaders, helping to shape the future of leadership practices.

Through Liddell Consulting Group, David offers services designed to empower business leaders to maximize their impact and achieve lasting success. With a focus on strategic growth, team development, and leadership excellence, David and his team work closely with clients to create tailored solutions that meet their unique challenges.

Learn more about how David can support your leadership journey by visiting **www.LiddellConsulting.com**.

www.ingramcontent.com/pod-product-compliance
Lightning Source LLC
Chambersburg PA
CBHW071858200326
41519CB00016B/4448